Hands-On Networking

with Internet Technologies

SECOND EDITION

Hands-On Networking

with Internet Technologies

SECOND EDITION

DOUGLAS E. COMER

Department of Computer Sciences
Purdue University
West Lafayette, IN 47907

Web site by W. DAVID LAVERELL

PEARSON
Prentice
Hall

Upper Saddle River, New Jersey 07458

Library of Congress Cataloging-in-Publication Data

CIP DATA AVAILABLE.

Vice President and Editorial Director, ECS: *Marcia Horton*
Publisher: *Alan Apt*
Associate Editor: *Toni Holm*
Editorial Assistant: *Patrick Lindner*
Vice President and Director of Production and Manufacturing, ESM: *David W. Riccardi*
Executive Managing Editor: *Vince O'Brien*
Managing Editor: *Camille Trentacoste*
Production Editor: *Irwin Zucker*
Manufacturing Manager: *Trudy Pisciotti*
Manufacturing Buyer: *Lisa McDowell*
Director of Creative Services: *Paul Belfanti*
Creative Director: *Carole Anson*
Art Director: *Heather Scott*
Cover Designer: *John Christiana*
Cover Art: *KJA-Artists.com*
Executive Marketing Manager: *Pamela Hersperger*
Marketing Assistant: *Barrie Reinhold*

© 2005, 2004, 2002 by Pearson Education, Inc.
Pearson Prentice Hall
Pearson Education, Inc.
Upper Saddle River, New Jersey 07458

Pearson Prentice Hall® is a trademark of Pearson Education, Inc.

TRADEMARK INFORMATION: Company and product names used in this text may be trademarks or registered trademarks of the individual companies, and are respectfully acknowledged. UNIX is a registered trademark of The Open Group in the U.S. and other countries. Microsoft Windows is a trademark of Microsoft Corporation. Solaris is a registered trademark of Sun Microsystems, Incorporated. Red Hat is a registered trademark and RPM is a trademark of Red Hat Incorporated. Linux is a registered trademark of Linus Torvalds.

Printed in the United States of America

10 9 8 7 6 5 4 3 2

ISBN 0-13-148696-9

Pearson Education Ltd., *London*
Pearson Education Australia Pty. Ltd., *Sydney*
Pearson Education Singapore Pte. Ltd.
Pearson Education North Asia Ltd. *Hong Kong*
Pearson Education Canada Inc., *Toronto*
Pearson Educación de Mexico, S.A. de C.V.
Pearson Education—Japan, Inc., *Tokyo*
Pearson Education—Malaysia Pte. Ltd.
Pearson Education Inc., *Upper Saddle River, New Jersey*

For Those Who Want An In-Depth
Understanding Of Computer Networking

Contents

Part II: Network Programming On A Set Of Shared Workstations

List Of Experiments

A Single Computer

Network Programming On A Set Of Shared Workstations

Measurement And Packet Analysis On Augmented Workstations

Configuration Experiments In A Dedicated Intranet Lab

Protocol Stack Implementation In A Special-Purpose Lab

System Design In A Network System Engineering Lab

Preface

Network engineers, managers, programmers, professors and students have all asked how they can gain a deeper understanding of computer networks and internets. This book answers the question. It asserts that the best way to learn is by doing — there is no good substitute for hands-on experience with a real network. Interconnecting hardware, configuring network systems, measuring performance, observing protocols in action, and creating client-server programs that communicate over a network all help sharpen one's understanding and appreciation.

What hardware and software facilities are required for hands-on experimentation? Instead of specifying an exact platform, this book is organized into six sections that each consider a hardware platform and outline experiments that can be carried out using the hardware. The first section begins by considering the smallest possible facility, a single stand-alone computer. Successive sections describe increasingly more powerful (and more expensive) facilities and the experiments they support. The last sections document advanced hardware and software facilities used for protocol development and network systems engineering. The point is that experimentation is always possible — although the facilities at hand determine the types of experiments that can be performed, even low-cost, general-purpose facilities offer opportunities.

The broadest distinction among facilities concerns isolation. Early sections of the book describe experiments that can be carried out on conventional, general-purpose computers connected to a production network. Later sections describe experiments such as packet capture, intranet configuration, and protocol development that require a special, dedicated facility. Industry often uses the terms *testbed* or *testnet* to describe a separate dedicated facility; academia usually uses the term *laboratory*. An industrial testbed can serve two purposes. Like an academic laboratory, a testbed provides an environment that supports training. In addition the testbed provides a safe environment in which new or upgraded network systems can be configured, measured, and tested before being installed in the company's production network. Although we use the academic term laboratory throughout the book, many of the experiments are designed with industrial testbeds in mind. In the section on configuration, for example, experiments specify using an isolated facility to configure hosts, routers, and a firewall to form an intranet.

In addition to a wide variety of topics, the experiments in this book cover a wide range of difficulty. Some experiments, especially those near the beginning of each chapter, are straightforward and may require less than a half hour to perform. Other experiments are both difficult and lengthy. For example, the IP router experiment described in Chapter 20 is taken from a second-year graduate class that I teach at Purdue. Students work in teams and require most of a semester to build a working IP router. Most experiments list optional extensions that suggest ways to go beyond the basics. The best students in my classes work through all the options, and sometimes invent options of their own.

Networking professionals who are working alone can pick and choose among experiments in various chapters. Programmers will focus on the client-server experiments in Parts I and II; system administrators will focus on the configuration experiments in Part IV. Engineers who implement and optimize network systems and protocol stacks will focus on the performance measurements in Part III or protocol development experiments in Parts V and VI.

Professors teaching networking courses can choose experiments appropriate to the class. Most colleges and universities cram all of networking and internetworking into a single one-semester overview course. In such a course, students should see a wide range of experiments to acquaint them with all aspects of the subject, especially network programming, network measurement, and protocol analysis. For example, students in my undergraduate class begin the first week using Internet applications and writing programs as described in Part II. When the lectures cover Local Area Networks, the students are assigned measurement experiments from Part III. The weeks that the lectures cover IP and TCP, students perform packet capture and protocol analysis experiments from Part III. Finally, students are ready to tackle a more advanced (socket) programming experiment from Part III.

Colleges and universities fortunate enough to have multiple courses in networking can divide the experiments in this book among the courses and go into more depth in each. In a one-semester network programming course students concentrate on the programming experiments in Part III. Students in such a course also enjoy building the internet emulation gateway from Chapter 8 and constructing a library for the simplified API. If students do not have any previous experience, they can begin by using the simplified API in Part II, which allows them to start programming before they learn the details of sockets. I usually encourage students in a network programming course to incorporate the optional extensions and to think about ways the software can be parameterized.

In a one-semester network administration course, students can focus on the configuration experiments in Part IV. Students enjoy creating their own version of an intranet, and are especially pleased when they can configure unconventional domain names. As an interesting challenge, I ask students to establish two apparently unrelated domain hierarchies for the same set of computers.

Finally, in any course that discusses protocol design, students should begin by building the Internet emulation gateway described in Chapter 8. The gateway project requires students to extend their knowledge of socket programming to include UDP, allows them to see an application gateway, and causes them to consider the possible errors with which protocols must contend (i.e., packet loss, duplication, corruption, and delay).

Several resources are available to aid those who want to establish a laboratory and try experiments. To aid experimenters we have established a companion web site for this book at:

www . labbook . cs . purdue . edu

The site contains sample output for the experiments, instructions for how to use specific compilers or operating systems, hints, and other helpful information. Experimenters, especially course instructors, are encouraged to contribute information to the site. W. David Laverell has agreed to manage the web site; David can be reached at:

lave @ calvin.edu

Many of the experiments reference my text *Computer Networks And Internets* for which there is both a web site:

www . netbook . cs . purdue . edu

and a mailing list:

netbook @ cs . purdue . edu.

To join the mailing list, send an email message *subscribe netbook* to

netbook-request @ cs . purdue . edu.

To leave the mailing list, send the email message *unsubscribe netbook* to the same address.

I gratefully acknowledge many years of support for my laboratories at Purdue from a variety of sources, including Agere Systems, Hewlett Packard, IBM Corporation, Intel Corporation, and Sun Microsystems. I especially thank the long list of graduate students who have contributed ideas and effort to the Xinu lab (described in Chapter 19) since its inception in 1984. I have not kept records, but I remember contributions from Bob Brown, Chris Kent, Steve Munson, Ken Rodemann, Raj Yavatkar, Andy Muckelbauer, Shawn Ostermann, John Lin, and Mike Evangelista. Most recently, Dennis Brylow, Ben Kupermann and Florian Kerschbaum ported the Xinu software to the latest set of back-end systems, including devising a device driver that works over a PCI bus; Dennis Brylow designed the reboot controller. Gustavo Rodriguez-Rivera helped with the lab management software, and Chris Telfer designed a next-generation facility that offers a GUI interface and automated interconnection. Special thanks go to my wife and partner, Christine, whose careful editing made many improvements throughout.

Douglas E. Comer

May, 2004

About The Author

Dr. Douglas Comer is an internationally recognized expert on TCP/IP protocols, computer networking, and the Internet. One of the researchers who contributed to the Internet as it was being formed in the late 1970s and 1980s, he was a member of the Internet Architecture Board, the group responsible for guiding the Internet's development. He was also chairman of the CSNET technical committee and a member of the CSNET executive committee.

Comer consults for industry on the design of computer networks. In addition to talks in universities, he teaches many onsite courses to networking professionals around the world. Comer's operating system, Xinu, and implementation of TCP/IP protocols (both documented in his textbooks) have been used in commercial products.

For many years, Comer has designed and built both networking testbeds and teaching laboratories. His work on laboratories was recognized when he was selected to serve on the ACM task force on core curricula. The task force followed his recommendation for laboratories in Computer Science and Computer Engineering curricula.

Comer is a distinguished professor of computer science at Purdue University, where he develops and teaches courses and does research on computer networking, internetworking, and operating systems. In addition to writing a series of highly acclaimed technical books that have been translated into sixteen languages, he serves as the North American editor of the journal *Software — Practice and Experience*. Comer is a Fellow of the ACM.

Additional information can be found at:

www.cs.purdue.edu/people/comer

and information about Comer's books can be found at:

www.comerbooks.com

Other Books In the Internetworking Series from Douglas Comer

Internetworking With TCP/IP Volume I: Principles, Protocols and Architectures, 4th edition: 2000, ISBN 0-13-01830-6

The classic reference in the field for anyone who wants to understand Internet technology, Volume I surveys the TCP/IP protocol suite and describes each component. The text covers protocols such as IP, ICMP, TCP, UDP, ARP, SNMP, and RTP, as well as concepts such as Virtual Private Networks and Address Translation.

Internetworking With TCP/IP Volume II: Design, Implementation, and Internals (with David Stevens), 3rd edition: 1999, ISBN 0-13-973843-6

Volume II continues the discussion of Volume I by using code from a running implementation of TCP/IP to illustrate all the details.

Internetworking With TCP/IP Volume III: Client-Server Programming and Applications (with David Stevens)
> **Linux/POSIX sockets version: 2000, ISBN 0-13-032071-4**
> **AT&T TLI Version: 1994, ISBN 0-13-474230-3**
> **Windows Sockets Version: 1997, ISBN 0-13-848714-6**

Volume III describes the fundamental concept of client-server computing used to build all distributed computing systems, and explains server designs as well as the tools and techniques used to build clients and servers. Three versions of Volume III are available for the socket API (Linux/POSIX), the TLI API (AT&T System V), and the Windows Sockets API (Microsoft).

Network Systems Design Using Network Processors, Intel IXP version: 2004, ISBN 0-13-141792-4

A comprehensive overview of the design and engineering of packet processing systems such as bridges, routers, TCP splicers, and NAT boxes. With a focus on network processor technology, *Network Systems Design* explains the principles of design, presents tradeoffs, and gives example code for a network processor.

The Internet Book: Everything you need to know about computer networking and how the Internet works, 3rd edition: 2000, ISBN 0-13-030852-8, paperback

A gentle introduction to networking and the Internet that does not assume the reader has a technical background. It explains the Internet in general terms, without focusing on a particular computer or a particular brand of software. Ideal for someone who wants to become Internet; an extensive glossary of terms and abbreviations is included.

To order, visit the Pearson Education Web page at www.pearsoned.com/ or contact your local bookstore or Pearson Education representative.

Hands-On Networking

with Internet Technologies

SECOND EDITION

1

Introduction And Overview

1.1 The Fundamental Need For A Laboratory

The Chinese have a proverb that is translated:

I hear and I forget,
I see and I remember,
I do and I understand.

The learn-by-doing approach is absolutely essential in computer networking. Although many college courses teach the protocols, technologies, and applications that underlie computer networks and internets, anyone who understands the field realizes that textbooks and lectures are an insufficient source of information — no book can provide complete insight into the subtleties or an appreciation of how the technologies operate in practice. Such insight can only be achieved through first-hand experience with computers connected by real network equipment. In short, deep understanding of networking requires laboratory facilities that allow one to build, observe, experiment, and measure. Hands-on access to a network reinforces concepts by forcing us to apply them and to achieve concrete results. As a result, laboratory experience allows us to see networking in action, to understand the functionality of each component, and to appreciate the subtleties.

1.2 The Spectrum Of Possible Lab Facilities

What equipment is needed in a hands-on networking laboratory and how much does it cost? How should equipment be interconnected? Surprisingly, the answer is that all lab experience — even experience with limited, inexpensive equipment — adds understanding. More sophisticated

1

equipment enables more sophisticated experiments. Thus, we will explore a spectrum of possible lab facilities that range from simple and inexpensive to complex and costly. For each lab facility, we will examine the hardware and software components required, consider how the equipment is interconnected, and list experiments that can be conducted on the facilities. We will learn that many experiments require only a small amount of inexpensive equipment, and that complex facilities are only needed for the most complex experiments.

Our exploration begins with a brief look at the simplest facility, a single computer, and its special role in helping develop and test network applications. We then focus on network programming, network packet analysis, and network configuration including an examination of lab facilities that support each activity. We will see that a lab to support network programming consists of multiple computers connected to a Local Area Network (LAN) and that a small amount of additional hardware must be added to support network packet analysis. A private intranet consisting of multiple LANs interconnected by routers is needed for experiments in network configuration. Later sections consider more sophisticated, special-purpose lab facilities with extensive and unusual functionality. One of the lab architectures we present offers experimenters† the ability to create and test a complete protocol stack; another offers experimenters the ability to work with network processors (special-purpose hardware devices used to build switches and routers).

The paragraphs below summarize the sequence of lab architectures we will consider, and characterize the set of experiments that are possible with each architecture. Later chapters of the book expand the lab descriptions and give more detail, including sets of experiments to be performed.

• The Simplest Facility: A Single Computer

The simplest facility that allows one to experiment with network software consists of a single computer. If it has Internet access, the computer can run applications that allow one to interact with Internet sites. Even if it does not have an Internet connection, a single computer can be used to develop and test network software by arranging for client and server applications to communicate within the single computer.

• A Typical Lab: Shared, General-Purpose Workstations

Typical laboratory facilities in a university are not dedicated to a single person, a single class, or a single use. Instead a lab for computer courses usually consists of general-purpose workstations that are shared among many students and classes. The computers in such a lab are interconnected by a Local Area Network; most labs also have a connection to the global Internet.

Shared facilities are ideal for experiments with client-server applications. Experimenters can use the lab for network programming: building and testing application-layer protocols. To test their software, an experimenter runs the client and server pieces on computers in the lab and allows them to communicate over the lab network. In addition to testing correctness, experimenters can measure performance.

---

†Throughout this text, we use the term *experimenter* to refer to anyone performing experiments, whether the person is a networking professional or a student enrolled in a course.

• An Inexpensive Upgrade: An Augmented, General-Purpose Facility

We will see that it is possible to augment a set of conventional workstations with inexpensive networking hardware that enables more sophisticated experiments, including packet capture and protocol analysis.

• A Configurable Lab: A Dedicated Intranet

An intranet facility consists of multiple networks interconnected by IP routers. When a dedicated intranet is available, it can be used to experiment with Internet address assignment and routing.

Unfortunately, few universities can afford a dedicated intranet facility for a student lab. We will see, however, that technologies like Network Address Translation (NAT) make it possible to perform some of the same experiments on shared facilities.

• For The Elite: A Specialized Protocol Development Lab

Perhaps the most interesting architecture described in the book consists of a highly specialized lab that has been in use at Purdue University for over a decade. The lab allows experimenters, working in teams, to build and test a complete TCP/IP protocol stack. To test their software, a team downloads a copy into one or more (otherwise idle) computers, and then arranges for the computers to communicate with one another, with conventional workstations in the lab, or with computers on the Internet.

• For Advanced Engineering: A Network Device Architecture Lab

Network devices such as bridges, switches, and routers are not built using conventional CPUs. Instead, they are constructed from special-purpose hardware such as programmable network processors. Learning to build high-speed network devices requires a lab that provides special-purpose hardware and software that allows experimenters to create microcode, download it into a programmable network processor, and measure / test the resulting system. The last section of the book considers such a lab.

1.3 A Word About Simulation

Throughout this book, we will emphasize first-hand experiments (i.e., experiments with real computers and real networks). Some instructors argue that it is better to use network simulators — large computer programs that mathematically model computer networks and protocols, and report how a given network would perform under load. The basic arguments in favor of simulators seem to be:

- Lower capital cost.
- Much easier to administer than a real network.
- Better protection because experiments cannot disrupt production networks.
- Ability to simulate gigantic networks (larger than can be found in a lab).

The first three arguments focus on what is easiest/best for the institution and lab administrator rather than what is best for the experimenter. Furthermore, we will see that the first argument is misleading — even a modest expenditure can result in interesting and useful lab facilities. Finally, the last argument only applies to the special case of advanced experimenters who already know basics. Most people learning networking are struggling to master basic concepts and to understand how networks operate; beginners are best served by labs where they can observe specific examples instead of simulators that hide many details. In short, a network simulator is an insufficient substitute for hands-on experience with real systems. Thus, whenever possible we will focus on experiments with standard protocols and actual networks. In cases where actual network facilities are unavailable or too expensive, we will concentrate on emulation rather than simulation — experiments will remain as close as possible to reality.

1.4 Organization Of The Book

The remainder of the book is organized into six major parts that each correspond to one of the architectures mentioned above. Each part begins with a detailed description of the architecture, including a description of the hardware and software components. It then characterizes the set of experiments that the architecture supports. Finally, the section concludes with a list of specific experiments that can be performed.

The lab writeup serves as both a guide to steps of the experiment and as a record of progress. To record progress, the experimenter checks off items as each is performed — when the experiment is complete, the page can be detached and handed in.

In terms of guiding one through the experiment, a writeup is divided into several sections. The writeup begins with a background reading section that lists references to consult and study before undertaking the lab. After a short overview, the writeup gives a detailed list of procedural steps to be carried out. Once a step has been completed, it should be checked off; if part of the work must be postponed until a later time, the record makes it easy to know exactly where to resume.

Experiments in the book are always ordered from simplest to most complex. For example, experiments listed for a given lab architecture are usually feasible on any of the more complex lab architectures that follow. Furthermore, chapters within a given architecture and experiments within a given chapter are listed in order from simplest to most complex. Usually, the first experiment in a chapter covers basic background material; we expect that it will be possible to conduct such experiments quickly with little or no outside help. However, some of the later experiments are advanced, and may require substantial time (e.g., some require most of a semester).

Finally, many experiments include a section labeled *Optional Extensions*. The section describes additional possibilities and shows interesting ways to extend the experiment. As the label implies, we do not suggest that everyone complete the optional extensions. Instead, we view them as challenges to illustrate how in networking it is always possible to look deeper — anyone who finds the basic experiments too easy will enjoy the optional extensions.

Part I
Network Programming
On A Single Computer

The Special Role Of
A Single Computer
In Experimental Networking

2

Hardware And Software On A Single Computer

2.1 The Two Types Of Support And Their Uses

A single computer can offer two levels of support that are important for networking:

- Support for access: TCP/IP software and a physical connection to the global Internet.

- Support for network programming: a compiler, an operating system that allows multiple applications to run concurrently, and support for Internet access.

The next chapter explains in more detail how each of these facilities is used. For now it is sufficient to know that support for network access makes it possible to execute standard applications that probe and measure the Internet, and support for network programming makes it possible to construct and test application programs that communicate over a network.

2.2 Support For Network Access

Most computers, even inexpensive models, offer support for network access. For example, a PC running one of Microsoft's Windows systems, a Unix system such as Solaris or Linux, or an Apple Macintosh running OS X all include the TCP/IP protocol software and applications needed to access the Internet. In each case, the user has a choice of a physical Internet connection: access over a dial-up telephone line or a direct connection through a Local Area Network interface (e.g., via cable modem or DSL).

2.3 Support For Network Programming

Network programming support is also broadly available. C compilers are available from multiple manufacturers for computers running Microsoft's Windows or Apple's OS X. The popular version of Linux, available from Red Hat, includes the Gnu C compiler.

In addition to a compiler, network programming also requires the operating system to provide an *Application Program Interface (API)* that allows applications access to protocol software in the operating system. Known as *sockets*, the most popular network API was originally developed for the Unix operating system. Linux contains one of the most extensive implementations of the socket API, which helps explain why Linux is popular among network programmers.

Because the socket API is so popular, most operating systems either offer the socket API directly or provide application programmers with a library that translates socket calls to the operating system's internal functions. For example, Microsoft developed a version of the socket API for its operating systems† that is known formally as *Windows Sockets* and is sometimes referred to as *WINSOCK*. However, a compiler does not always provide Windows Sockets functions automatically; a program that uses them must be linked with the Windows Sockets library (*wsock32.lib*).

2.4 Recommendations

If you have a choice, we recommend choosing a computer that runs the Linux operating system. See

http://www.linux.org/

for general information about Linux, including links to user groups and distribution sites. You can find information about the popular Red Hat distribution at:

http://www.redhat.com/

2.5 Summary

Most computer systems include support for network access, including TCP/IP protocol software and dial-up or direct network connections. Support for network programming is also widely available. Operating system vendors and third parties sell compilers for the C programming language; most operating systems also offer the necessary Application Program Interface (API). Linux, which is especially popular among network programmers, includes TCP/IP protocol support, a C compiler, and an extensive implementation of the socket API.

---

†Technically, the Windows Sockets API depends on the *WIN32* systems interface.

3

Experiments Using Application Programs

3.1 Using A Single Computer To Experiment With Applications

A single computer with Internet access can be used to experiment with application layer protocols. For example, most computer systems include application programs such as *ping* and *traceroute* (which is also called *tracert* on some systems) that can be used to probe the Internet. Ping, which tests whether a specified destination is reachable, allows the user to specify an argument that causes ping to measure the delay to the site. Traceroute records the set of intermediate routers along the path to a specified site.

One of the most useful experimental tools is a program named *telnet*. Originally designed as a client for the Internet remote login service, telnet provides basic functionality that can be used to experiment with a variety of application protocols. Telnet connects a user's keyboard and screen to an application service on a remote computer — everything the user types is sent to the remote computer, and everything the remote computer generates is displayed on the user's screen. Thus, telnet allows a user to fill the role of a client application. For example, one of the experiments in this chapter illustrates how telnet can be used to contact an email server and transfer an email message, which the server will then deliver to the specified user.

3.2 Using A Computer To Develop And Test Network Applications

Surprisingly, an individual computer — even a stand-alone computer that does not have any network connection — plays an important role in network programming. Individual computers help in two ways. First, a computer that has support for networking programming allows programmers to build application programs that interact with network protocol software. The experimenter can learn about the network API by building and running applications that use it. Second, once network application software has been created, an experimenter needs to perform extensive *interoperability testing*. Using multiple computers for debugging is time-consuming because the experimenter must copy the software to each computer, and must then ensure that the applications communicate with one another. If instead of using multiple computers the experimenter tests the software on a single computer, debugging proceeds much faster.

How can network applications communicate on a single computer? The answer lies in *loopback addressing* facilities provided by protocol software†. A packet marked for loopback never travels across a network. In fact, a loopback packet never leaves the local computer. Instead, the internet-layer software, known as *IP*, intercepts the outgoing packet and delivers it back to the transport software on the local machine.

Loopback is important for testing network applications because loopback does not require modification to the application software. Instead, an application is built to use the standard network API (i.e., the API used to communicate with an application on a remote computer). To perform loopback testing, the programmer specifies the loopback destination. The protocol software on most computers recognizes the special domain name, *localhost*, which it translates to the reserved IP address 127.0.0.1.

Recall that applications communicate in pairs, with members of the pair known as a *client* and a *server*. Figure 3.1 illustrates communication within a single computer using loopback testing. As the figure shows, both the client and server programs run on the same computer at the same time. In this case, the client has used a loopback address to form a TCP connection to the server on the same computer. When the client sends data across the connection, TCP places the data in a segment, wraps the segment in an IP datagram, and forwards the datagram to the IP layer. Because the datagram is destined to the loopback address, IP sends the datagram back to TCP, which delivers it to the server. Similarly, when the server sends data, the protocol software delivers the data to the client.

3.3 Stress Testing Applications With An Emulated Internet

Although most Internet applications use reliable transport (i.e., TCP), some are designed to use unreliable transport (i.e., UDP). In the latter case, the application protocol must be designed to handle the problems of packet loss, duplication, delay, and reordering, all of which can occur in the Internet. A modified form of loopback testing, also performed on a single computer, can be used to test whether an application can handle such problems.

---

†We recommend using loopback testing on a single computer for an initial interoperability test whenever building a network application; all the network programming experiments in Part II recommend using a loopback test.

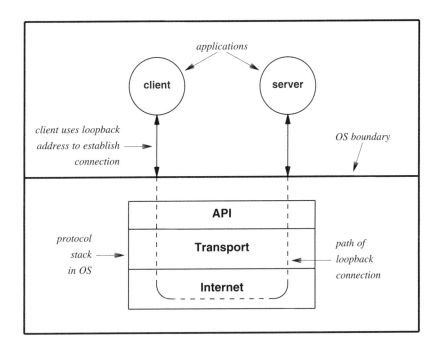

Figure 3.1 Illustration of loopback testing on a single computer. Two applications running on the same computer communicate as if they were running on two separate computers. Protocol software in the operating system passes packets back up the stack without sending them over the network.

Known as *stress-testing*, the procedure requires an intermediary between the client and server. The programmer arranges to send all communication between the client and server through the intermediary. To emulate a wide-area Internet environment, the intermediary artificially introduces packet problems. That is, the intermediary is programmed to randomly discard, duplicate, corrupt, delay, or reorder packets as they pass through.

When a single computer is used for stress-testing, the intermediary is implemented as an *application gateway* program. Thus, to perform stress testing on a single computer, a programmer runs three programs concurrently. Figure 3.2 illustrates the concept, and shows how the underlying protocols are used.

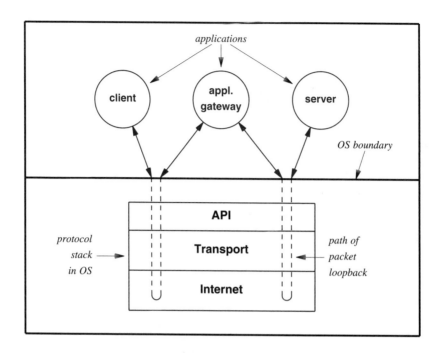

Figure 3.2 Illustration of stress-testing on a single computer. An application gateway acts as an intermediary between a client and server, and introduces random packet errors.

To ensure that the gateway can be used in a variety of tests, it must be possible to choose error rates. Typically, the application gateway is programmed to read a configuration file that specifies a probability for each type of packet problem. For example, if the configuration file specifies 2% packet loss, the application gateway uses probability of .02 to randomly discard packets. Under Unix systems, the gateway can be programmed to read the configuration file when it receives a signal, meaning the error rate can be changed quickly. For example, after measuring the interaction between a client and server for one error rate, the experimenter only needs to change the configuration file and signal the gateway to measure the client and server at another error rate.

What addresses do a client, server, and intermediate gateway use? Both the intermediate gateway and the server are reached using the special loopback address: *localhost*. To prevent ambiguity, the gateway and server are each assigned a separate transport protocol port number. For example, suppose the server operates on UDP port 20000. The gateway can be assigned 20001. The client is temporarily directed to port 20001, and the gateway is programmed to forward packets that arrive from the client to port 20000. Thus, when it receives a packet from the client, the gateway applies the probabilistic rules for errors and then forwards the data from the packet to the server. When it responds, the server sends a reply to the gateway, which then creates a new packet and responds to the client†.

---

†Chapter 8 includes an experiment that asks experimenters to build an application gateway that can be used for stress testing.

3.4 Transport Protocol Development On A Single Computer

The configuration illustrated in Figure 3.2 provides an excellent testbed for experiments with transport protocols. In addition to emulating packet errors, the gateway can be programmed to emulate a network that has a low capacity (e.g., a 64 Kbps connection). In essence, the gateway delays each packet the amount of time that would be consumed when sending the packet over the low-capacity line. That is, to emulate a line of data rate D, the gateway computes T, the number of milliseconds that would elapse when sending the packet at D bits per second. The gateway then delays the packet T milliseconds before forwarding.

3.5 Summary

A single computer can be used to probe the Internet using widely available utility programs such as *ping* and *traceroute*. Programs such as *telnet* allow a computer to be used for experiments with application protocols that use ASCII encoding. A single computer provides an ideal environment for network software development and testing. Programmers perform initial interoperability tests on a single computer by running both the client and server applications on the same computer. To allow the two programs to communicate, the programmer specifies the special computer name *localhost* or uses the reserved IP loopback address. The applications then use TCP/IP protocols to communicate even though the packets do not pass across a network.

A single computer can also be used for stress-testing network applications. To perform a stress test, packets are sent through an intermediary that is implemented as an application-layer gateway. The gateway emulates a wide area Internet environment by randomly dropping, duplicating, delaying, reordering, or corrupting packets. The gateway can also emulate a low-throughput network by computing the rate at which to forward packets.

Name: _____

Experiment 3.1
Use Telnet To Contact A Fortune Server

Purpose

To understand how application layer protocols use an ASCII encoding for messages, and how to use telnet as a tool to experiment with such protocols.

Overview

Use the *telnet* program to contact a fortune server and request a fortune. The server will not know that a human controls one end of the connection; you must follow the application protocol exactly. That is, once a connection has been established to the server, you must enter keystrokes exactly as the server expects.

Procedure And Details (checkmark as each is completed)

_____ 1. Determine how to run the *telnet* program on your local computer. Usually, telnet takes two command-line arguments: the name of a remote computer to contact, and an integer port number that specifies an application on the remote computer.

_____ 2. Run telnet and contact port 8445 on computer *cookie.update.uu.se*. On many computers, the appropriate command consists of:

```
telnet cookie.update.uu.se  8445
```

_____ 3. Verify that telnet displays status messages such (e.g., *Trying...*, *Connected...*, and *Escape...*).

_____ 4. Enter a single line that contains the integers 1 and 10:

```
1   10
```

_____ 5. Verify that the server returns a fortune and closes the connection (i.e., after displaying the fortune, the telnet program exits).

_____ 6. Contact the site repeatedly, and verify that the fortune changes for each contact.

Optional Extensions (checkmark options as they are completed)

_____ 7. Read *http://www.update.uu.se/cookie.html* to learn more about the fortune cookie data-
base.

_____ 8. If you are using a Unix system, write a shell script that invokes telnet, sends the line containing two integers, and displays the output without the telnet control messages.

Notes

Experiment 3.2
Use Telnet To Contact A Web Server

Purpose

To understand how application layer protocols use an ASCII encoding for messages, and how to use telnet as a tool to experiment with such protocols.

Background Reading And Preparation

Read Chapters 35 and 3 in *Computer Networks And Internets* to learn about the HTTP protocol used with the World Wide Web and how web servers are implemented.

Overview

Use the *telnet* program to contact a web server and request a page. The server will not know that a human controls one end of the connection; you must follow the application protocol exactly. That is, once a connection has been established to the server, you must enter keystrokes that follow the protocol (HTTP).

Procedure And Details (checkmark as each is completed)

_____ 1. Determine how to run the *telnet* program on your local computer. Usually, telnet takes two command-line arguments: the name of a remote computer to contact, and an integer port number that specifies an application on the remote computer.

_____ 2. Run telnet and contact port 80. For example, on many computers, the appropriate command consists of:

```
telnet www.labbook.cs.purdue.edu  80
```

_____ 3. Enter the following text:

```
GET  http://www.labbook.cs.purdue.edu  HTTP/1.0
```
   ← *you must enter a blank line here*

_____ 4. Verify that the server returns an HTML document, and then closes the connection (i.e., after displaying the page, the telnet program exits).

_____ 5. Contact another web site, and obtain a copy of a web page.

Optional Extensions (checkmark options as they are completed)

_____ 6. If you are using a Unix system, write a shell script that invokes telnet, sends a request, and displays the output without the telnet control messages.

_____ 7. Write a Unix shell script that uses telnet to obtain a copy of a web page, and place the copy in a file.

Notes

Experiment 3.3
Use Telnet To Send An Email Message

Purpose

To understand how application layer protocols use an ASCII encoding and how to use telnet as a tool to experiment with such protocols.

Background Reading And Preparation

Read Chapter 32 in *Computer Networks And Internets* to learn about SMTP and email.

Overview

Use the *telnet* program to contact an email server and transfer a message. The server will not know that a human controls one end of the connection; you must follow the application protocol exactly. That is, once a connection has been established to the server, you must enter keystrokes that follow the protocol (SMTP).

Procedure And Details (checkmark as each is completed)

_____ 1. Determine how to run the *telnet* program on your local computer.

_____ 2. Determine the domain name of your local computer, call it L. If you are at a university, the name will have a form similar to

$$mycomputer.cs.myuniversity.edu$$

_____ 3. Find M, the domain name of a computer that runs an email server. If your personal workstation runs an email server, use *localhost* as the name, otherwise, choose a computer in your organization.

_____ 4. Use telnet to contact the email server on computer M. Typically, telnet takes two arguments on the command line: the name of the computer to contact and the integer 25, which denotes the email service. The server will respond by sending an identification.

_____ 5. Enter the following text (the server will respond to each command):

        HELO *fill in the local domain name, L, here*
        MAIL FROM: a_networking_guru
        RCPT TO: *fill in a target email address here (e.g., your own email address)*
        DATA
           fill in a message here. The body of the message
           can span multiple lines of text.
        .   *←Type a period on a line by itself to terminate the message.*
        QUIT

_____ 6. Verify that the server closed the connection (i.e., that the telnet program exits).

_____ 7. Verify that the mail server delivers the message to the specified recipient.

Optional Extensions (checkmark options as they are completed)

_____ 8. If you are using a Unix system, write a shell script that invokes telnet, and sends a mail message without displaying telnet control messages.

_____ 9. Specify multiple *RCPT TO:* lines before entering the message, and verify that each receives a copy.

_____ 10. Generate a mail message with bogus "from" information (i.e., replace *a_networking_guru* with an arbitrary string), send the message to your email account, and verify that a copy arrives.

_____ 11. Some mail servers require the *HELO* line to authenticate the sender. See if you can find a mail server that does not require HELO.

Name: _____

Experiment 3.4
Use The Ping Program

Purpose

To test the Internet connection between two computers.

Background Reading And Preparation

Read Chapter 2 in *Computer Networks And Internets* to learn about ping.

Overview

Use the *ping* utility to determine reachability to a set of computers.

Procedure And Details (checkmark as each is completed)

_____ 1. Determine how to run the *ping* program on your local computer.

_____ 2. Find a help page that lists the flags and arguments to the *ping* program and explains each.

_____ 3. Ping *localhost* to determine that the ping program is working; ping should report that the destination is alive.

_____ 4. Choose a well-known site such as *www.google.com*, and use ping to determine if the site is reachable.

_____ 5. Use a search engine to find the domain name of a computer in another country, and ping the computer. What is the largest round-trip time you can find?

Optional Extensions (checkmark options as they are completed)

_____ 6. Find an option that allows ping to send probe packets repeatedly (flag *-s* on some Unix systems), and ping a remote site 100 times. Report the number of packets lost as a percentage of total packets sent.

_____ 7. If your computer system allows multiple application programs to run concurrently, ping four sites separately and then at the same time to determine whether the round-trip times differ.

Notes

Name: _____

Experiment 3.5
Download And Use A Packet Capture Tool

Purpose

To learn how a packet capture tool works. Packet capture is especially useful when debugging network applications, so mastering the use of a packet capture tool will be especially helpful with later experiments.

Background Reading And Preparation

Read Chapter 9 in *Computer Networks And Internets* to learn about packet capture tools.

Overview

Download a packet capture tool from the Internet, and run it on the local computer.

Procedure And Details (checkmark as each is completed)

_____ 1. Go to Web site *www.ethereal.com*, which offers a shareware version of a packet capture and analysis program that works over Ethernet, and download a copy onto your local computer.

_____ 2. Run the Ethereal application to capture 100 packets, and save the results in a file.

Optional Extensions (checkmark options as they are completed)

_____ 3. If you have a Wi-Fi interface, enable the Wi-Fi interface, and use Ethereal to capture packets from a Wi-Fi network.

_____ 4. Allow Ethereal to run for a while, and collect statistics. What percentage of the packets on your network are broadcast packets?

_____ 5. Allow Ethereal to run for a while, and make a list of all packet types that Ethereal finds on your network.

Notes

Part II
Network Programming
On Shared Workstations

Experiments That Involve Building Client-Server Software And Testing The Software On A Set Of Workstations

4

Hardware And Software For A Shared Workstation Lab

4.1 Consequences Of Sharing

Most educational institutions cannot afford to build a lab for each course. Instead, they provide a general-purpose computational facility that must be shared — the lab is reserved for a specific class at specific times during the week. Because they are shared, the lab facilities must support a wide variety of uses. Each workstation is a general-purpose computer that runs a multi-user operating system that is configured with an account for each user. More important, experimenters are not permitted to install new hardware, modify the operating system, or reboot the computer.

The network in a shared lab must also be restricted. Most labs use a Local Area Network (LAN) to interconnect computers; the lab may also have a router that provides a connection to the global Internet. Because the lab is shared among many users, however, the network carries production traffic. For example, packets may contain passwords, work by other users, or other confidential data†. Consequently, experimenters cannot be permitted to capture packets from the lab network or transmit arbitrary packets across the network.

4.2 Example Shared Lab Technologies

- *Workstation Hardware.* Almost any general-purpose computer can be used in a shared lab. At the high end, for example, Hewlett Packard Corporation makes an Alpha computer. Sun Microsystems makes inexpensive Sparc computers. Many educational institutions choose Intel architecture PCs because they also have low cost.

---

†Although encryption can be used to keep data confidential, it is often unreasonable to demand that all data in a laboratory be encrypted.

- *Network Hardware.* Although it is possible to use other network technologies, most educational labs use Ethernet because it provides high capacity at extremely low cost. For example, Ethernet switches are available for 100 or 1000 Mbps (Fast Ethernet or Gigabit Ethernet).

- *Protocol Software.* Almost everyone uses TCP/IP protocols (the protocols used on the Internet).

- *Operating System.* To some extent, the operating system depends on the hardware. Typical systems include Linux, Sun Microsystems' Solaris, or any of Microsoft's Windows systems; each is available for computers that use the Intel architecture (e.g., a PC).

4.3 Architecture Of A Shared Lab

Most shared labs have a straightforward architecture as Figure 4.1 illustrates.

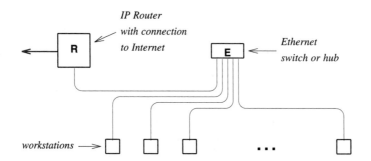

Figure 4.1 The physical connections among equipment in a general-purpose lab that can be shared among many users. Each workstation attaches to a Local Area Network; an IP router connects the lab to the rest of the Internet†.

An Ethernet switch or hub, *E*, forms the central interconnect in the shared lab. Each workstation attaches to the switch over a twisted pair cable, as does the router, *R*.

4.4 Using A Shared Lab In A Networking Course

A lab of workstations connected by a LAN provides an ideal environment for network programming. Experimenters can build application programs that communicate across the LAN from one computer to another, can master an API such as sockets, and can test their

---

†In practice, the Internet connection can be protected by a security firewall.

software on a real network. More important, the close proximity of computers in a lab makes it easy to perform experiments on multiple computers.

4.5 Broadcast Domain Assumption

In some of the experiments that follow, we will assume that the lab consists of a single *broadcast domain*. That is, we assume a broadcast or multicast packet can be sent by any computer and all computers in the lab receive a copy. Because it provides a single broadcast domain, a conventional switch or a conventional hub follows our assumption. A *Virtual LAN* (*VLAN*) switch can be configured to provide multiple broadcast domains. If the lab administrator has chosen to partition the lab into multiple broadcast domains, experimenters must find a subset of the computers that lie in a given broadcast domain and perform the experiment on that subset. Mapping the broadcast domains of computers is one possible experiment.

4.6 Summary

The most widely-available lab facilities consist of shared workstations connected by a Local Area Network, possibly with an IP router that provides a connection to the global Internet. A shared lab provides an excellent environment for network programming. Experimenters can build and test application software that communicates across the network between two computers.

5

Network Programming Experiments Using A Simplified API

5.1 Introduction

The experiments that follow all use the simplified network API described in Chapter 3 of the text *Computer Networks And Internets*. Anyone unfamiliar with the API should read the chapter which contains a detailed description of the API, describes its use, and shows example code. The figures below merely provide a quick reference.

The simplified API consists of the seven functions listed in Figure 5.1.

Operation	Meaning
await_contact	used by a server to wait for contact from a client
make_contact	used by a client to contact a server
cname_to_comp	used to translate a computer name to an equivalent internal binary value
appname_to_appnum	used to translate a program name to an equivalent internal binary value
send	used by either client or server to send data
recv	used by either client or server to receive data
send_eof	used by both client and server after they have finished sending data

Figure 5.1 The seven functions that comprise the simplified API used for experiments in this chapter.

The first two functions initialize communication. To form a connection, a server calls *await_contact* and a client calls *make_contact*. Once a connection is in place, either end can call *send* to transmit data and *recv* to receive data. When they finish, each side calls *send_eof*. After both sides call *send_eof*, the connection is broken and communication is terminated. Finally, the API includes two functions to translate from a text string to an internal binary value. Function *cname_to_comp* translates from a computer's domain name to the computer's address, and *appname_to_appnum* translates the name of a service to the corresponding binary value.

The API defines several data types. Types *computer* and *appnum* define binary values used internally. Type *connection* defines the type of the value returned when a connection is formed; to transfer data over the connection, the value must be passed to the *send* function. Figure 5.2 summarizes the data types of the arguments and the return value of each function.

Function Name	Type Returned	Type of arg 1	Type of arg 2	Type of args 3 & 4
await_contact	connection	appnum		
make_contact	connection	computer	appnum	
appname_to_appnum	appnum	char *		
cname_to_comp	computer	char *		
send	int	connection	char *	int
recv	int	connection	char *	int
send_eof	int	connection		

Figure 5.2 The data types of functions in the API.

5.2 Obtaining Software For The API

The API has been tested on both Windows as well as on Unix systems. The software is available from the web site for *Computer Networks And Internets*:

http://www.netbook.cs.purdue.edu

Experimenters who use Windows must obtain individual files from the web site, and build a compilation environment (i.e., define a "project" for the compiler). Experimenters who use a Unix system can download a complete tar file of all the API software and examples with subdirectories for compiling under Linux or Solaris from:

ftp://ftp.cs.purdue.edu/pub/comer/netbook/CNAI.api.tar

5.3 Summary

Experiments in this chapter use a simplified API that allows a programmer to create network applications without understanding many details. Software for the API is available for use with Windows or a Unix operating system.

Experiment 5.1

Compile, Test, And Extend Example Echo Software

Purpose

To learn how to compile, link, run, and modify a computer program that communicates over the Internet.

Background Reading And Preparation

Read about the simplified network programming API in Chapter 3 of *Computer Networks And Internets*. Note especially the description of the *echo* client and server. Find out how to compile C language programs on your local computer system, and how to link a binary with the API library and the system's socket library. (Note: although you will not use sockets directly, the API code depends on sockets.)

Overview

Compile and test a copy of the echo client. Then compile a copy of the echo server, run the two programs on separate computers, and verify that they can communicate.

Procedure And Details (checkmark as each is completed)

_____ 1. Obtain a copy of the code for the API, the echo client, and the echo server†.

_____ 2. Compile and link the echo client with the API library and the socket library.

_____ 3. Test the echo client. A server is not needed for testing because the *echo* service is standard throughout the Internet. Thus, to test the client, specify the name of a computer in your lab and the standard application number for echo, 7.

_____ 4. Compile and link the server.

---

†Details about obtaining the API can be found in Section 5.2 on page 32.

_____ 5. To test the server, you will need a unique *application number*. If multiple groups are using a lab, it will be necessary for each running server to be assigned a unique number. Have your instructor assign you a unique number or coordinate among yourselves to choose the next unassigned value starting at 20001, 20002, 20003, and so on. Record the number on the line below.

_____

_____ 6. Perform a loopback test with the client and server running on one computer as described in Chapter 3 of this text. Use the computer name *localhost* and the application number that was assigned to your server in the previous step.

_____ 7. Test the client and server by running the server on one computer and the client on another.

Analysis

_____ 8. We said that many computers offer an echo service. If other groups are also running servers, a client may appear to work even if it has contacted the wrong server. To ensure that a client is interacting with the specified server, run the server, run the client, and then while they are interacting kill (abort) the server process.

Optional Extensions (checkmark options as they are completed)

_____ 9. Modify the server to keep a log file containing all data the server echoes.

_____ 10. The server has been designed to accept contact from a client, handle the contact, and then exit. Modify the code so that after handling a given client, the server waits for contact from another client.

Experiment 5.2
Compile, Test, And Extend Example Chat Software

Purpose

To learn how to modify and extend application programs that communicate over the Internet.

Background Reading And Preparation

Read about the simplified network programming API in Chapter 3 of *Computer Networks And Internets*. Note especially the description of the *chat* client and server.

Overview

Compile a copy of the chat client and server programs, and test to ensure they can communicate. Extend the programs so they accept a user name when they start up, and prepend the user name to each line they send.

Procedure And Details (checkmark as each is completed)

_____ 1. Obtain and compile a copy of the chat client and server software. Use the API and socket libraries.

_____ 2. To test a server, you will need a unique *application number*. If multiple groups are using a lab, it will be necessary for each running server to be assigned a unique number. Have your instructor assign you a unique number or coordinate among yourselves to choose the next unassigned value starting at 25001, 25002, 25003, and so on†. Record the number on the line below.

_____

_____ 3. Perform a loopback test of the client and server on a single computer (see Chapter 3 of this text for details). Use the computer name *localhost* and the application number that was assigned to your server in the previous step.

---

†In principle, an experimenter can retain the same application number from one experiment to the next; we recommend choosing a unique application number for each server to make it possible to run the servers simultaneously.

_____ 4. Test the software on two computers to ensure that the client and server communicate.

_____ 5. Modify the client and server so they each require the user to enter a "name" (an arbitrary string). Prepend the name followed by a greater-than sign to each line of text before sending the text across the network.

_____ 6. Test the modified version of the code.

Output

Lines displayed from the remote user will each begin with the user's name.

> Chris> Hello there.
> Chris> Are we having fun yet?

Optional Extensions (checkmark options as they are completed)

_____ 7. Sending the remote user's name with each line of text wastes network bandwidth. Modify the program so the name is only sent once by arranging for the first line sent across the network to contain the user's name. Have the receiving side remember the name and prepend the name to each line of output.

_____ 8. The chat program waits for an entire line of text before sending anything across the network. Modify the code so instead of waiting, one side sends each individual keystroke and the other side displays characters as they arrive. Use the *select* function to determine whether the local user has typed a character or a character has arrived from the remote site.

_____ 9. Build a chat system that divides the screen into two separate areas, and displays local keystrokes in one area and characters received from the other side in the other area.

_____ 10. Add a timer to the chat program so that the TCP connection is automatically closed after three minutes of idle time (i.e., three minutes during which no characters are sent or received).

Experiment 5.3
Build A Simple File Transfer Service

Purpose

To learn the basics of file transfer and how to build a client and server that interoperate.

Background Reading And Preparation

Read about the simplified network programming API in Chapter 3 of *Computer Networks And Internets*.

Overview

Build a file transfer service that consists of a client and server. Have the server export a set of files from the computer on which it runs (i.e., make them available for download), and have the client obtain a file on demand. That is, arrange to have the client send a file name and for the server to respond by sending the file.

Procedure And Details (checkmark as each is completed)

_____ 1. Specify the exact details of the file transfer protocol, including the line terminator.

_____ 2. Consult the examples in Chapter 3 of *Computer Networks And Internets* to see what arguments the client and server programs will need, and specify the arguments you will use.

_____ 3. Write, compile, and link a file transfer server, *ftserve*, that waits for a connection, receives a file name, opens the named file, sends the file contents back over the connection, and then sends an end-of-file. Have the server exit after sending one file.

_____ 4. Write, compile, and link a file transfer client, *ftclient*, that forms a connection to the server, sends the file name, and displays the retrieved file on the screen.

_____ 5. To test the server, you will need a unique *application number*. If multiple groups are using a lab, it will be necessary for each running server to be assigned a unique number. Have your instructor assign you a unique number or coordinate among yourselves to

choose the next unassigned value starting at 27001, 27002, 27003, and so on. Record the
number on the line below.

_____

_____ 6. Using the application number that was assigned to your server in the previous step, perform a loopback test on a single computer as described in Chapter 3 of this text. Transfer
an ASCII text file.

_____ 7. Test the client and server on two separate computers.

Optional Extensions (checkmark options as they are completed)

_____ 8. Modify the client so it places the retrieved data in a local disk file that has the same name
as the remote file.

_____ 9. Modify the server so that instead of exiting after sending one file, it runs continuously,
waiting for new connections and sending a file for each connection.

_____ 10. Extend the protocol to permit the client to send a *GET* command followed by a file name
or by a *LIST* command that requests a list of all the files the server offers.

_____ 11. Extend the file transfer client and server to allow interactive access (i.e., a user invokes
the client and then enters a series of commands).

_____ 12. Add a configuration file to the server that provides a mapping between a set of virtual file
names and the actual files on the server's computer. Make all interaction with the client
use the virtual file names.

_____ 13. Add encryption to the client and server so that the data passing between them is encrypted.

6

Network Programming Experiments Using The Socket API

6.1 Introduction

The experiments in this chapter all use the socket *Application Program Interface* (*API*). The socket API, which was originally developed for the UNIX operating system, is available on most platforms, and has become the de facto standard for network programming.

6.2 Information About Sockets

Information about sockets is widely available. Several texts describe the functions that comprise the socket API and provide examples of how sockets are used to build client and server software. Read Chapter 29 of *Computer Networks And Internets* for a general description of sockets along with an example client and server. For details about sockets in the Linux operating system (along with many examples of clients and servers) consult *Internetworking With TCP/IP Volume 3: Client-Server Programming and Applications (Linux/POSIX edition)*. For the same examples built to use Microsoft's version of sockets, read *Internetworking With TCP/IP Volume 3: Client-Server Programming and Applications (Windows Sockets Version)*.

Information about socket functions can also be found on the World Wide Web. However, because it provides authoritative answers for the version of sockets available to you, the vendor's information should be used to resolve all questions about function declarations and data types.

In addition to learning how to call specific socket functions, you will need to learn how to create an executable binary that uses socket functions. For example, in most systems a program that uses sockets will not compile correctly unless the source file has additional *#include* statements to inject socket declarations. Furthermore, once a program has been compiled, the resulting binary must be linked with a socket library. In Unix systems, the library is specified with a -*l* option to the *cc* or *gcc* command; in Windows, the library is specified with a / option. The vendor's documentation specifies the include statement(s) needed in source programs and the libraries that must be used when the binary is linked.

6.3 A Note About The Difficulty Of Socket Programming

Although sockets form an important part of network programming, socket programming is not easy. First, because the API contains many functions, a client or server must make many calls. Second, using the socket functions requires attention to details such as byte order. Thus, even basic socket programming can be overwhelming.

To learn about sockets, we recommend starting with running code and modifying it slowly. For example, Experiment 6.2 (the first experiment that involves socket programming) suggests starting with an existing echo client and echo server. It is easiest to replace one function call at a time and test the result before proceeding to replace other calls.

6.4 Summary

Experiments in this chapter use the socket API, which has become a de facto standard for network programming. Because it contains many functions and involves many details, programming with the socket API is much more difficult than programming with the simplified API described in previous chapters. Although general descriptions of socket functions are available, the vendor's documentation provides the most authoritative information on how to use a specific API.

Experiment 6.1
Compile, Link, And Run A Socket Program

Purpose

To learn how to compile, link, and run a computer program that uses the socket API.

Background Reading And Preparation

Follow the references given at the beginning of this chapter to learn about socket API in general. Consult the vendor's documentation, as needed, to determine which include files are required for compilation of a program that uses sockets and how to link a binary with the socket library. Read about the example client and server in Chapter 30 in *Computer Networks And Internets*.

Overview

Obtain, compile, and test a copy of client and server software that uses the socket API.

Procedure And Details (checkmark as each is completed)

_____ 1. Download a copy of files *client.c* and *server.c* from the FTP site given in the following URL:

ftp://ftp.cs.purdue.edu/pub/comer/netbook/

_____ 2. Compile the client, and link the resulting binary with the socket library.

_____ 3. Perform a loopback test of the client on the local computer as described in Chapter 3 of this text. To perform the test, use the *DAYTIME* port (i.e., port 13).

_____ 4. Compile the server, and link the resulting binary with the socket library.

_____ 5. A unique protocol port number will be needed to test a server. Obtain a value from your instructor, or coordinate among others in the lab by choosing a value from the sequence 23001, 23002, 23003, and so on. Record the number on the line below.

_____

_____ 6. Perform a loopback test by running both the client and server on the local computer.

_____ 7. Test the client and server by running them on two computers.

Analysis

Not all computers offer the *DAYTIME* service. What happens if the argument to the client specifies a computer that does not run a *DAYTIME* server?

Optional Extensions (checkmark options as they are completed)

_____ 8. If your system has the *make* utility, build a *Makefile* that contains all commands needed to compile and link the client and server.

_____ 9. Source code for programs such as *traceroute* that use the socket API can be found on the web. Download and compile source code for a well-known program.

Notes

Experiment 6.2
Write An Echo Client And Server Using Sockets

Purpose

To learn how to create client and server software using the socket API.

Background Reading And Preparation

Follow the references given at the beginning of this chapter to learn about socket API in general. Consult the vendor's documentation, as needed, to determine which include files are required for compilation of a program that uses sockets and how to link a binary with the socket library. If necessary, study the example client and server code in Chapter 30 of *Computer Networks And Internets*.

Examine the description of the *echo* client and server in Chapter 3 of *Computer Networks And Internets*. Although the code uses the simplified API, the basic operation and structure of the programs will remain the same when modified to use sockets.

Overview

Obtain a copy of the echo client and server software that uses a simplified API, rewrite the software to use the socket API, and test the resulting client and server†.

Procedure And Details (checkmark as each is completed)

_____ 1. Rewrite the *echo* client program to use the socket API. Specify connection-oriented communication (i.e., the TCP protocol). Once a connection has been established, the client repeatedly reads a line of input from the user, sends the line to the server, receives the reply from the server, and displays the reply as output to the user.

_____ 2. Perform a loopback test with the echo client on the local computer by specifying protocol port 7 (the port reserved for the *ECHO* service) and computer *localhost*.

---

†Note for less experienced programmers: as described in section 6.3, it is easiest to perform this experiment in stages, replacing and testing one function at a time.

_____ 3. Rewrite the *echo* server program to use the socket API. The server waits for a TCP connection and then repeatedly reads a line of text from the connection and sends the line back to the client.

_____ 4. To test the server, you will need a unique *protocol port number*. If multiple groups are using a lab, it will be necessary for each running server to be assigned a unique port. Have your instructor assign you a unique number or coordinate among yourselves to choose the next unassigned value starting at 20001, 20002, 20003, and so on. Record the number on the line below.

_____

_____ 5. Perform a loopback test on the local computer by specifying your assigned protocol port and, for the client, computer name *localhost*.

_____ 6. Test the client and server on two computers.

_____ 7. Verify that the client works if the server receives and sends at most ten characters at a time (i.e., restrict the buffer to ten characters).

Optional Extensions (checkmark options as they are completed)

_____ 8. When an error occurs, most implementations of the socket functions return a value of -1 and set a global value, *errno* to indicate the exact error. Determine how the version of sockets you are using returns error status, and print detailed error messages.

_____ 9. The well-known protocol ports have each been assigned a name as well as a number. For example, the name *echo* has been assigned to port 7. Extend the client and server so the argument specifying a protocol port can be either a name or a number.

_____ 10. The server has been designed to accept contact from a client, handle the contact, and then exit. Modify the code so that after handling a given client, the server waits for contact from another client.

Experiment 6.3
Build A Web Server Using Sockets

Purpose

To learn how to build a web server that correctly interoperates with a browser.

Background Reading And Preparation

Examine the simple web server in Chapter 3 of *Computer Networks And Internets*. If you need information about the *HyperText Transfer Protocol* (*HTTP*) that browsers and servers use to communicate, look at Internet RFC 1945. Internet RFCs are available from many sources, including the CD-ROM that comes with *Computer Networks and Internets*. If you do not have RFCs available, they can be acquired from the web. Start with:

http://www.rfc-editor.org/

Overview

Build and test a web server that returns a page in response to a request from a browser.

Procedure And Details (checkmark as each is completed)

_____ 1. Design a mapping from document names to files. Each GET request sent to the server will have the form:

GET *SP* Document_Name SP** HTTP/1.0 *CRLF*

where *SP** denotes one or more blank characters, *Document_Name* is a string that identifies a particular document your server offers, and *CRLF* denotes the two characters *carriage return* and *linefeed*. HTTP/1.0 is an example of a version number. Typically, all documents are placed in a single directory in the server's file system, and *Document_Name* merely gives a path within that directory.

_____ 2. Build a basic web server using the socket API. The server should passively wait for a TCP connection, read and parse the HTTP *GET* request, return the requested page, and close the connection.

_____ 3. To test a server, you will need a unique *protocol port number*. If multiple groups are using a lab, it will be necessary for each running server to be assigned a unique number. Have your instructor assign you a unique number or coordinate among yourselves to choose the next unassigned value starting at 29001, 29002, 29003, and so on. Record the number on the line below.

_____ 4. Perform a loopback test on your server by using a browser. Give the browser a URL for the local computer with the protocol port set to the number you have been assigned and the path corresponding to a valid document. For example:

http://localhost:29001/document1

_____ 5. Test your server across the lab network by running the browser and server on separate computers.

Optional Extensions (checkmark options as they are completed)

_____ 6. A client can send additional information following a *GET* request. The additional information is terminated by a blank line (i.e., the occurrence of four consecutive characters: *CR LF CR LF*). Arrange for your server to ignore the additional information.

_____ 7. Modify your server to handle errors gracefully. If a browser requests a file that does not exist, the server should return the following sequence of lines (each line is terminated by the two-character sequence *CRLF*):

```
HTTP/1.0  404 File Not Found   CRLF
Server:  server_type   CRLF
Content-type:  document-type   CRLF
CRLF
<Other error information>
```

_____ 8. Extend the server to allow it to browse a directory. When the *path* given in the *GET* request corresponds to a directory, generate a list of files in the directory, add HTML tags to format the list, and return the result to the browser.

_____ 9. Modify the server to handle dynamic pages. When the *path* corresponds to an executable program, run the program and send the output back to the browser. For additional ideas, consult the Common Gateway Interface (CGI) standard:

http://hoohoo.ncsa.uiuc.edu/cgi/

_____ 10. Read about an HTTP 302 message, and add a capability to your server that forwards requests that it cannot handle to another server.

Experiment 6.4
Build A Library For A Network API

Purpose

To learn how to construct a network library that hides the details of sockets.

Background Reading And Preparation

Read about the simplified network programming API in Chapter 3 of *Computer Networks And Internets*. Follow the references given at the beginning of this chapter to learn about socket API in general.

Overview

Implement and test a library of functions that comprise a network API.

Procedure And Details (checkmark as each is completed)

_____ 1. Extend the API from *Computer Networks And Internets* to include functions that support connectionless communication (i.e., communication through sockets that use UDP). Define each function in the API, the type of each argument, and the type the function returns.

_____ 2. Use sockets to implement the extended API. Implement each function.

_____ 3. Test the connection-oriented functions in the API that are used by a client. To do so, compile and run one of the client programs in Chapter 3 of *Computer Networks And Internets*.

_____ 4. Test the connection-oriented functions in the API that are used by a server. To do so, compile and run one of the server programs in Chapter 3 of *Computer Networks And Internets*.

_____ 5. Test the connectionless functions in the API. To do so, build a client and a server program that use connectionless communication.

Optional Extensions (checkmark options as they are completed)

_____ 6. Extend the API to provide a way to pass back a detailed error message to the calling application.

_____ 7. Add API support for applications that use IP multicast.

Notes

7

Concurrent Network Programming Experiments

7.1 Introduction

The experiments in previous chapters focused on the basic form of client-server interaction in which one client communicates with one server at a time. This chapter expands the scope of network programming experiments to include *concurrent execution*, a topic that is fundamental in network programming. Concurrent execution is especially pertinent for servers because it permits a single server to handle requests from multiple clients at the same time. In fact, without concurrent execution, large-scale Internet web sites would not be possible.

Operating systems offer two forms of concurrency: multiple *threads of execution* and multiple *processes*. In the experiments that follow, we will see that a server can use either form that an operating system supports.

In addition to depending on the operating system at hand, the choice of concurrency also depends on the application for which a server is being created. For example, threads are needed for servers that allow clients to modify and control shared state information because only threads allow concurrently executing copies of a program to share memory. Processes are required for servers that need to execute one of several external programs because only a separate process can replace itself with an external program. There are other differences between the two styles of concurrent execution. Process creation generates more overhead than thread creation. However, threads incur overhead when they change global (shared) data because such changes must be coordinated among all threads.

7.2 Summary

Experiments in this chapter explore the use of concurrent execution with network applications. Concurrency is especially important in servers because it permits large scale. Operating systems offer two basic forms of concurrency: threads and processes. Both forms of concurrency can be used with network applications.

Name: _____

Experiment 7.1
Build A Concurrent Server (Threads)

Purpose

To learn how to create a server capable of handling connections from multiple clients concurrently.

Background Reading And Preparation

Before beginning this experiment, you should understand how to write a program that uses threads for concurrent execution. You should also have code for a server (e.g., a web server or a file transfer server). If you have not constructed a server, refer to Experiment 6.3 that starts with the basic web server described in Chapter 3 of *Computer Networks And Internets* and extends it to handle files.

Read Chapters 11 and 12 in *Internetworking With TCP/IP Volume 3: Client-Server Programming And Applications*† to understand how servers use concurrency and how to construct a concurrent server using threads.

Overview

Modify and test your server to make it capable of handing multiple connections concurrently.

Procedure And Details (checkmark as each is completed)

_____ 1. You will need a unique protocol port number to test a server. Obtain a value from your instructor, or coordinate among others in the lab by choosing a value from the sequence 29001, 29002, 29003, and so on. Record the number on the line below.

_____

_____ 2. Compile and test the server to ensure it works properly.

---

†Two versions of the text are available. Unix users should read the *Linux/POSIX version* and Microsoft users should read the *Windows Sockets version*.

_____ 3. Divide the code for the server into two parts, a main program, M, and a procedure, P. Arrange for the main program to accept an incoming connection and call procedure P. Pass the descriptor for the connection as an argument to the procedure. The procedure should perform the same action on the connection as the server originally performed (e.g., read a request and send a response).

_____ 4. Rewrite the main program, M, so that instead of calling procedure P directly, the program creates a thread to execute P. That is, M will consist of an infinite loop that receives the next connection, creates a thread to handle the connection, and then continues waiting for the next connection.

_____ 5. Start the server and perform a loopback test. Arrange for a client to send a request, and verify that the server responds correctly.

_____ 6. Extend the loopback test by trying to send multiple requests sequentially. That is, leave the server running and run the client several times; make one request each time.

_____ 7. Perform a loopback test of concurrency by running two copies of the client simultaneously. Have one of the clients issue a request for a large item (e.g., a large GIF image). While the first client is being served, have the second client issue a request for a small item (e.g., a small text file), and verify that the second request completes while the first continues to run.

_____ 8. Perform a concurrent test of the server using three machines, one for the server and one for each of the two clients.

Optional Extensions (checkmark options as they are completed)

_____ 9. Devise an experiment to find out how many concurrent TCP connections your operating system supports.

_____ 10. Modify the server to keep a log of connection requests along with the number of simultaneous connections. What is the maximum number of connections you can achieve in the lab?

Experiment 7.2

Build A Concurrent File Transfer Server (Processes)

Purpose

To learn how to use separate processes to allow a server to handle multiple clients concurrently.

Background Reading And Preparation

Before beginning this experiment, you should understand how to write a program that creates multiple concurrent processes†. You should also have built a file transfer server and a client to test it.

Read Chapter 11 in *Internetworking With TCP/IP Volume 3: Client-Server Programming And Applications (Linux/POSIX version)* to understand how servers use concurrency and how to construct a concurrent server using processes.

Overview

Construct a file transfer server that spawns a separate process to handle each incoming connection.

Procedure And Details (checkmark as each is completed)

_____ 1. You will need a unique protocol port number to test a server. Obtain a value from your instructor, or coordinate among others in the lab by choosing a value from the sequence 27001, 27002, 27003, and so on. Record the number on the line below.

_____

_____ 2. Compile and test your file transfer client and server programs to ensure they work properly.

---

†This experiment is designed for a Unix environment, where process creation is straightforward (i.e., it does not work well in a Microsoft environment).

_____ 3. Divide the code for the server into two parts, a main program, M, that manages incoming connections and a separate procedure, P, that handles a single connection. Arrange for the main program to accept an incoming TCP connection and call procedure P. The procedure should interact with the client according to the application protocol (e.g., respond to a request by sending the requested file). Do not pass the socket descriptor of the connection as an explicit argument to procedure P. Instead, build the procedure to assume the socket descriptor is zero, and have the main program use primitives such as *dup* to move the descriptor for the incoming connection to zero before calling the procedure. Test the resulting code.

_____ 4. Rewrite the main program so instead of calling procedure P directly, the program calls an operating system function such as *fork* or *ProcessCreate* to spawn a new process each time a connection arrives. Arrange for the new process to handle the connection and exit. Arrange for the main program, M, to continue in an infinite loop that waits for a new connection and creates a process to handle the connection.

_____ 5. Start the server and use the client to perform a loopback test. Execute a single file and verify that the server handles it correctly.

_____ 6. Extend the loopback test by trying to retrieve multiple items sequentially. That is, leave the server running, and request items one at a time.

_____ 7. Perform a loopback test of concurrency by running two copies of the client simultaneously. Have one of the clients issue a request for a large item (e.g., fetch a large file). While the first client is being served, have the second client issue a request for a small item (e.g., a small text file), and verify that the second request completes while the first continues to run.

_____ 8. Perform a concurrent test of the server using three machines, one for the server and one for each of the two clients.

Optional Extensions (checkmark options as they are completed)

_____ 9. Implement a concurrent version of the file transfer server using threads, and compare the performance of the two versions.

_____ 10. If you are using a variant of the UNIX operating system, read about zombie processes and modify the server to clean up zombies. (Hints: (1) the main server process receives a signal whenever a child process exits; (2) the *wait* function must be called when a child exits.)

Experiment 7.3
Build A Multiservice Server

Purpose

To learn how a single server can handle multiple services and execute separate programs

Background Reading And Preparation

Before beginning this experiment, you should understand how to write a program that creates multiple concurrent processes (i.e., Unix *fork*) and how a process can overlay itself with new code (i.e., Unix *exec*). You should also have built a concurrent server that spawns a separate process for each connection. Finally, you should have the code for at least two services (although we will use *echo* and *file transfer* in the description that follows, other services can be substituted).

Read Chapter 15 in *Internetworking With TCP/IP Volume 3: Client-Server Programming And Applications (Linux/POSIX version)*, or Chapter 14 in the *Windows Sockets version*, to understand how a single server can handle multiple services.

Overview

Construct and test a single, concurrent server that offers both an echo service and a file transfer service.

Procedure And Details (checkmark as each is completed)

_____ 1. You will need at least two unique protocol port numbers to test a multiservice server, one for each service being offered. Obtain two values from your instructor, or coordinate among others in the lab by choosing two values from the sequence 25001, 25002, 25003, and so on. Record the numbers on the lines below.

_____   _____

_____ 2. Compile and test the client and server programs for the two services to ensure they work properly.

_____ 3. Transform each server into a procedure that will be called by a main server program. Assume that a socket is already connected before the procedure is called.

_____ 4. Build a server program to manage connections. The program starts by opening two sockets, one for each service, and then enters an infinite loop. Inside the loop, use the *select* function to wait for one of the sockets to become ready, and call the *accept* function on that socket to accept the incoming connection. Finally, use *dup* to move the socket descriptor to descriptor zero, and create a process to handle the client. The new process should execute a procedure that corresponds to the requested service, and then exit.

_____ 5. Perform a loopback test with the server and the two clients. Test one service and then the other.

_____ 6. Extend the loopback test by trying to access the two services simultaneously. That is, run the two clients simultaneously. Have one of the clients issue a request that takes a long time. While the first client is being served, have the second client issue a request that takes a short time, and verify that the second request completes while the first continues to run.

_____ 7. Perform a concurrent test of the server by using multiple instances of clients for each service.

Optional Extensions (checkmark options as they are completed)

_____ 8. Extend the server to make it *multiservice* (e.g., make the server capable of handling 16 services instead of two).

_____ 9. Extend the server to handle multiple transport protocols (e.g., implement an echo service for UDP as well as an echo service for TCP).

_____ 10. Read about the Unix program *inetd*, and build your own version of inetd.

8

Protocol Design Experiments

8.1 Introduction

Previous chapters focus on building applications that communicate over an internet — the experiments all assume a conventional internet is in place with TCP/IP protocols to provide applications with a reliable, flow-controlled communication channel. This chapter considers the design of the protocols themselves. The experiments allow experimenters to design protocols, implement the resulting design, and perform a stress test with the resulting system.

8.2 Stress Testing Protocols

Stress testing is the most important part of protocol testing. Realistic testing requires a mechanism that can introduce errors similar to the errors that occur in a production internet: packet loss, duplication, corruption, and out-of-order delivery. The first experiment in this chapter asks the experimenter to design and implement such a mechanism: an *application gateway* that provides Internet emulation. Once such a gateway is in place, additional experiments ask experimenters to design protocols and then use the gateway to verify that the protocols will work across an Internet.

8.3 Internet Emulation With A Gateway

The basic concept of stress testing is discussed in Chapter 3 which illustrates how an application gateway program and *loopback* can be used to provide stress testing on a single computer. Two applications are built that implement a protocol, and then the applications are tested by having all communication pass through the gateway. The gateway emulates Internet error conditions by randomly dropping, delaying, duplicating, or corrupting data packets as they pass through.

The first experiment in this chapter extends the architecture used for stress testing in a significant way. To make the emulation gateway general, the suggested design does not restrict testing to a single computer (i.e., does not rely on *loopback*). Instead, the gateway can run on one computer in the lab and allow a pair of programs running on two other computers to exchange messages. More important, the suggested design does not restrict communication to a single pair of applications — multiple sets of applications can use the gateway at the same time.

Figure 8.1 illustrates the architecture and shows the path of communication between two application programs. One application sends a message to the gateway, which forwards it to the other application.

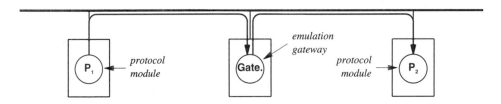

Figure 8.1 Illustration of an Internet emulation gateway used to stress test protocol software. As messages flow through it, the gateway introduces packet errors.

8.4 Emulation Behavior

We said that the application gateway should emulate Internet behavior, which means that the gateway should randomly drop, duplicate, corrupt, and delay packets. However, many questions remain. Which packets should the gateway drop? How much delay or data corruption should a gateway inject? Should the gateway emulate average-case Internet behavior or worst-case behavior?

From a testing perspective, another question arises: should the gateway always introduce errors at exactly the same point in the communication stream or should the errors occur at random? There are two conflicting goals. On one hand, to permit a programmer to test, modify, and then retest applications under the same conditions, a gateway must behave exactly the same way from one test to the next. On the other hand, if the gateway always introduces exactly the same packet errors on each run, testing will not be exhaustive (i.e., problems may remain hidden).

The dilemma can be solved using a *configurable* gateway that offers both options. Moreover, to make a configurable gateway usable for rapid testing, it should be designed so the behavior can be changed without recompiling the code. Each time a pair of applications uses the gateway to communicate, they specify to the gateway whether errors should be injected at exactly the same places as during the previous test or whether errors should be injected at random. Furthermore, a gateway that allows the applications to determine its probabilistic behavior will permit emulation of various Internet environments. For example, parameters can be set to specify that the gateway should emulate a slow network (e.g., one with a throughput of 56 Kbps), or to specify the probability with which the gateway will drop, duplicate, delay or corrupt packets. In addition, it should be possible to specify additional details such as the maximum delay the gateway adds to any packet.

8.5 Gateway Details

UDP Protocol. To ensure that the emulation gateway can be used to test protocol software without interference, communication between the gateway and applications must use a mechanism that sends and receives individual messages without buffering or flow control. Among the Internet protocols, UDP offers the required datagram service. Thus, all messages sent between the gateway and application programs will use UDP.

Single Protocol Port Number. Interestingly, we will see that a gateway using UDP needs only a single protocol port for all communication. Both applications send to the same port; the gateway uses the source address in each incoming packet to demultiplex.

Registration. Because it uses one protocol port for all communication, the gateway must be configured to know the addresses of the two applications as well as other parameters. Our gateway uses a straightforward mechanism: when an application begins, the application sends the gateway a single *registration* message that specifies the needed parameters. The gateway records the address and protocol port information associated with each registration message so it knows how to reach the application. Once a gateway has received registration messages from both ends, the gateway responds by sending a *confirmation* message to each endpoint. As soon as it receives a confirmation, an application can proceed to send messages through the gateway to the application on the other end.

8.6 Gateway Registration Message

Our gateway uses a simple rule to recognize a registration message: the incoming packet must begin with the ASCII string *%%%GatewayRegistration*. The remainder of the packet, also in ASCII, consists of text lines separate by the ASCII *NEWLINE* character. Each line specifies a parameter. The line begins with a keyword followed by one or more values. The table in Figure 8.2 lists the possible parameters.

%%%GatewayRegistration	*endpoint unique_name*
through	*throughput of the emulated network in Kbps*
delay	*delay of the emulated network in milliseconds*
dupl	*percentage of packets to duplicate*
drop	*percentage of packets to drop*
jitter	*percentage of packets to delay max_jitter*
corrupt	*percentage of packets to corrupt percentage of bits*
timeout	*value in milliseconds*
seed	*integer seed for pseudo-random numbers*

Figure 8.2 Format of a registration message sent to the Internet emulation gateway. The message is represented in ASCII.

Shared Workstation Lab

The first line of the message contains two pieces of information: an *endpoint* specification and a *unique name*. The endpoint specification consists of the string `client` or the string `server`†. Requiring an application to identify itself as one endpoint or the other helps catch errors such as cases where a programmer accidentally starts two copies of the same application.

The gateway uses the *unique name* on a registration message to determine which applications belong to a pair; only applications that supply the same unique name in their registration can communicate. The gateway does not interpret the contents of the unique name, so any string is allowed. In a multi-user environment, for example, the unique name might consist of a user's last name. Alternatively, each user can be assigned a unique integer.

The *through* and *delay* values are optional. If given, *delay* specifies the delay of the emulated network, and *through* specifies the throughput of the slowest network. The gateway delays each packet *delay* milliseconds. In addition, the gateway further delays each packet the time that would be required to send the packet across a network with the specified throughput (i.e., delay is proportional to packet size). The delay and throughput values make it easy to emulate most networks (e.g., a 56 Kbps satellite link).

Lines that specify packet errors should be obvious. For example, a line that begins with the keyword *dupl* contains an integer between 0 and 100 that specifies the percentage of packets to duplicate. Similarly, *drop* and *corrupt* specify the percentage of packets to discard and bits to change. The gateway converts the value to a probability between zero and one, which it then uses to randomly duplicate packets. Duplication is performed before other operations, which means that one copy of a duplicated message might be corrupted while another copy passes through unchanged. The *jitter* specification causes the gateway to add a random amount of extra delay to randomly selected packets (the percentage of packets to select and the maximum extra delay are both specified).

The *timeout* value is used to provide *soft state* for the gateway. A registration request that specifies a timeout of N seconds allows the gateway to cancel the registration if no activity occurs for a period of N seconds. Thus, a timeout can be used to automatically cancel a registration after a test completes. Timeouts also apply to registrations that never complete (i.e., one side registers, but the other does not).

The gateway uses the *seed* value to initialize the pseudo-random number generator. If no seed is given, the gateway uses the current time as a seed. Thus, if the same seed is given, the gateway will repeat the same behavior on successive tests.

8.7 Packet Exchange

Communication among the two applications and the gateway proceeds as Figure 8.3 illustrates.

---

†Although the terms *client* and *server* may not apply in some cases, they are easier to remember and use than more generic terms such as *side1* and *side2*.

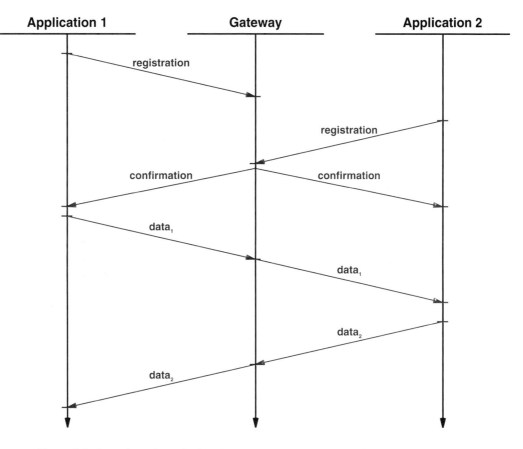

Figure 8.3 Illustration of a typical packet exchange among two applications and an Internet emulation gateway. After both applications register, the gateway sends a confirmation message to each and they can begin exchanging data.

As the figure shows, whichever application begins first (typically the side acting as a server) uses UDP to send a registration message to the gateway, and waits for a reply. The gateway does not respond immediately, but waits instead for the second application to register. The registration remains in limbo until the second application acts. The second application also uses UDP to send a registration message to the gateway, and waits for a reply. The gateway uses the unique name on an incoming request to match pairs of messages and complete the registration. As soon as a registration completes, the gateway sends both sides a confirmation message, which indicates that the applications may begin exchanging data. The confirmation consists of a UDP packet that contains a single line of text encoded in ASCII. Figure 8.4 illustrates the format.

%%%GatewayConfirmation   *date*

Figure 8.4 Format of a confirmation message that the Internet emulation gateway sends after a pair of programs have completed registration. Each side receives such a confirmation.

The confirmation is terminated by an ASCII *NEWLINE* character. The *date* field, which gives the current time and date on the gateway computer, can be used to verify that the message is current.

8.8 Error Processing

The diagram in Figure 8.3 shows the messages that should be exchanged during registration. If an error occurs, however, the gateway sends a message to indicate the exact error. The error message consists of a UDP packet that contains a single line of text encoded in ASCII. A numeric *error code* indicates the cause of the error, and the gateway can choose to provide additional text describing the problem. Figure 8.5 illustrates the error message format.

%%%GatewayError   *error code   optional explanation*

Figure 8.5 Format of an error message that the Internet emulation gateway sends.

The table in Figure 8.6 lists the possible error codes and the meaning of each.

Error	Meaning
1	Syntax error in registration request
2	Illegal configuration value
3	Timeout
4	Non-control message sent before registration complete

Figure 8.6 The possible error codes and their meanings.

8.9 Gateway Semantics And Defaults

Observe that each application sends a registration message, and each registration can specify parameters independently. The gateway applies the parameters from a registration request only to packets traveling *to* the application. It may seem odd that each end must specify parameters independently. After all, most networks are symmetric — the throughput is the same in both directions. We have chosen to separate the specifications to allow emulation of an asymmetric network. For example, ISPs that supply downstream delivery via satellite often use an alternative path (e.g., dialup) for upstream traffic. Because it permits separate parameters for each direction, our gateway can emulate such an architecture.

How should the gateway handle messages if neither registration message specifies any parameters? Our gateway merely passes messages through without any delay or change. That is, in the absence of parameters, the gateway emulates a default network that has zero delay and jitter, infinite throughput, and no packet errors. Although it does not provide any stress, the default configuration permits programmers to verify that they have established communication before they attempt to conduct a stress test.

8.10 Possible Extensions

As described, our gateway requires each side to send all parameters explicitly when registering. In many cases, it is convenient to assign a name to a set of parameters and to refer to the set by name. For example, suppose an instructor chooses to specify a set of parameters that all students must use for testing. It is also useful to have a set of parameters predefined for standard networks (e.g., parameters for a geo-stationary satellite).

Our gateway can easily be extended to accommodate named sets of parameters. Assume that each set of parameters is placed in a separate file in a well-known directory. The registration message can be extended by adding the name of the file to the first line.

%%%GatewayRegistration *endpoint   unique_name   parameter_file*

When the gateway receives such a registration, it opens the parameter file and treats the specification as if it had been present in the registration message. Thus, the mechanism is simply a shorthand that saves replicating parameters on each message.

8.11 Summary

Protocol design experiments require a facility that can be used for stress testing. To be general, such a facility must be able to emulate conventional network characteristics such as delay and throughput as well as random error conditions such as packet duplication, loss, random delay, and corruption.

We have described an application gateway approach that provides Internet emulation. The gateway allows a pair of applications to register for service. During registration, each side specifies the parameters desired; the two applications then exchange packets, and the gateway introduces random duplication, delay, loss, and corruption, as specified.

Experiment 8.1
Build An Internet Emulation Gateway

Purpose

To learn how an Internet emulation gateway operates and to build a useful tool for protocol experiments.

Background Reading And Preparation

Read the description of the emulation gateway at the beginning of this chapter.

Overview

Construct and test an emulation gateway. Because remaining experiments in this chapter use the gateway built in this experiment, it is important to test the gateway carefully.

Procedure And Details (checkmark as each is completed)

_____ 1. You will need a unique protocol port number to test a gateway. Obtain a value from your instructor, or coordinate among others in the lab by choosing a value from the sequence 25000, 25001, 25002, and so on. Record the number on the line below:

_____

_____ 2. Construct a preliminary piece of the gateway by building an application that creates a UDP socket using your assigned protocol port number, listens for an incoming message, and prints the IP address and protocol port number of the sender.

_____ 3. Write a test application that creates a UDP socket and sends a message to the gateway, and verify that it prints the correct address.

_____ 4. Extend the gateway to receive registration requests from two applications and place their address information in a table, and send each a confirmation. Use the table to forward messages from one application to the other.

_____ 5. Extend the application so it sends data, and test that the gateway can forward data.

_____ 6. Extend the gateway to parse a registration message, extract the parameters, and send an appropriate error message if a specification is incorrect.

_____ 7. Implement procedures that randomly duplicate, drop, and corrupt messages according to the parameters.

_____ 8. Extend the gateway to add delay and jitter. Note: it may be easiest to use multiple threads to handle delay.

_____ 9. Extend the gateway to handle timeout of idle registrations.

Optional Extensions (checkmark options as they are completed)

_____ 10. Extend the error messages to include a more detailed description of the error.

_____ 11. Implement named sets of parameters as described earlier in the chapter.

_____ 12. Create a new message type and extend the gateway to allow one application to *reregister* (i.e., change the parameters on the fly) without requiring the other application to change.

_____ 13. Add a logging facility that the gateway uses to record all registration, timeout, and error events.

_____ 14. Add a facility to simulate congestion by varying the delay over time. Arrange for a cycle of increase and decrease to repeat over time.

_____ 15. Extend the congestion simulation in the previous option to include variation of the packets dropped (e.g., arrange for the percentage of packets dropped to increase and decrease during the cycle).

Experiment 8.2
Design A Clock Synchronization Protocol

Purpose

To learn how to build a protocol that synchronizes clocks in two computers that are separated by a network.

Background Reading And Preparation

In *Computer Networks And Internets* read about network delay and jitter in Chapter 15, and look at the code for an echo client and server in Chapter 3.

Overview

Devise, implement, and test a protocol for clock synchronization (i.e., a protocol that allows a pair of applications to communicate across a network and computes the difference in the time of day reported by the clocks on the two computers).

Procedure And Details (checkmark as each is completed)

_____ 1. Devise a protocol used by a pair of applications to compute the network delay between them. Assume the network delay in one direction is one-half the round-trip time, and compute the round-trip time by arranging for one application to send a message to which the other application responds.

_____ 2. Implement the protocol and compute the network delay between two programs.

_____ 3. Test the two applications by using the Internet emulation gateway described in this chapter to introduce delay. Run the experiment with emulated delays of 0, 50, 100, 150, and 200 milliseconds.

_____ 4. Extend the protocol so that in addition to measuring delay, the application also sends the local time and date across the network. On the receiving side, add the estimated network delay to the timestamp in the incoming packet and compare the result to the local time. Repeat the measurement fifty times and print the average of differences in the clocks.

_____ 5. Use the Internet emulation gateway described earlier in this chapter to test performance of the program with delays of 0, 50, 100, 150, and 200 milliseconds.

Optional Extensions (checkmark options as they are completed)

_____ 6. Extend the protocol to handle a network that introduces jitter. Instead of measuring one round-trip time, arrange for each application to take many measurements and then compute a mean. Similarly, instead of sending the time once, arrange for each application to send the time repeatedly and compute a mean. Use the emulation gateway with and without jitter to test the protocol.

_____ 7. Devise a more sophisticated protocol that can be used with an *asymmetric* network (i.e., a network in which the delay in one direction differs from the delay in the other).

Notes

Experiment 8.3
Design A Reliable Data Transfer Protocol

Purpose

To learn how a protocol can provide reliable delivery over an unreliable network.

Background Reading And Preparation

Read Chapters 7, 16, and 25 in *Computer Networks And Internets* to learn about techniques such as checksums, packet sequence numbers, and retransmission that protocols use to detect or correct problems (e.g., bit errors, missing packets, or packets that arrive out-of-order).

Overview

Devise, implement, and test a protocol that provides reliable data transfer across a network that drops, delays, or corrupts packets.

Procedure And Details (checkmark as each is completed)

_____ 1. Implement two applications that use UDP to exchange messages. Verify that the applications can communicate through an Internet emulation gateway (use the default gateway semantics with no errors or delays).

_____ 2. Devise a protocol that uses a checksum and sequence numbers to handle corrupted and duplicated packets (i.e., define a message header). Have the sender place a sequence number and checksum in the header of each outgoing packet. Have the receiver use the checksum to verify that the packet arrives intact and the sequence number to remove duplicates.

_____ 3. Use the emulation gateway to test the protocol by transferring a large volume of data (i.e., many packets). Specify a high percentage of duplicates and a nonzero value for corruption.

_____ 4. Extend the protocol to handle packet loss by arranging for the receiver to return an acknowledgement. Have the sender retransmit a packet if the acknowledgement does not arrive within 50 milliseconds. Wait for successful acknowledgement of each packet before sending the next.

_____ 5. Use the emulation gateway to test retransmission by specifying a nonzero drop rate and transferring a large volume of data.

_____ 6. Test the protocol with simultaneous duplication, packet loss, and packet corruption.

Optional Extensions (checkmark options as they are completed)

_____ 7. Implement a CRC instead of a checksum, and measure the difference in CPU use as well as the difference in data throughput.

_____ 8. Experiment with the retransmission timer to find the smallest timeout that does not generate unnecessary retransmissions.

Notes

Experiment 8.4
Design A Sliding Window Protocol

Purpose

To learn how to build a protocol that uses the sliding window technique for flow control.

Background Reading And Preparation

Read about the sliding window technique for flow control in Chapter 16 of *Computer Networks And Internets*.

Overview

Devise, implement, and test a protocol that uses sliding window flow control.

Procedure And Details (checkmark as each is completed)

_____ 1. Implement two applications that use UDP to exchange data, and verify that the applications can communicate through an Internet emulation gateway (use the default gateway semantics with no errors or delays).

_____ 2. Devise a protocol that can be used to send a large volume of data (e.g., a file) in small messages (e.g., no more than 1K data octets per message). Define a message header that allows the sender to place a 16-bit sequence number in each outgoing message, and allows the receiver to return an acknowledgement number when a message arrives. Also include a bit in the header to indicate the last packet (i.e., end-of-file).

_____ 3. Implement the protocol with two application programs. Have the sender wait for an acknowledgement to arrive for message K before sending message $K+1$. Test the resulting programs.

_____ 4. Extend the protocol to use a sliding window scheme with a window size of 8 messages.

_____ 5. Implement the modified protocol. To verify that the sliding window works, have the sender display a log of incoming and outgoing packets. Test the resulting software.

_____ 6. Configure the emulation gateway with a high delay on the path from the receiver to the sender, and verify that a full window of messages can be transmitted before an acknowledgement arrives.

_____ 7. Compare the throughput of a protocol that uses sliding window to a version of the protocol that does not.

Optional Extensions (checkmark options as they are completed)

_____ 8. A 16-bit sequence number limits transmission to 2^{16} messages with unique sequence numbers. Revise the protocol to work correctly using a 5-bit sequence number (i.e., allow the sequence numbers to wrap around).

_____ 9. Instead of using a constant window size of 8, revise the programs so the window size is a parameter. Plot a graph of throughput for window sizes of 4, 8, 16, 32, 64, and 128.

_____ 10. Assume that a connection has a long duration, and build a protocol that dynamically varies the window size to find an optimal value (i.e., find a size, W, such that further increases do not produce higher throughput).

Notes

Experiment 8.5
Debug An Application Protocol

Purpose

To learn how TCP operates and how implementation details of a transport protocol affect the design of an application protocol.

Background Reading And Preparation

Read about TCP in Chapter 25 of *Computer Networks And Internets*.

Overview

Build a client and server that simultaneously transmit data in two directions, and find cases under which the application fails.

Procedure And Details (checkmark as each is completed)

_____ 1. Implement a client and server that form a TCP connection, and arrange for each side to (1) send an ASCII identification string, (2) call *shutdown* to mark the end of the transmission, and (3) read and display the identification string sent by the other side. For example, arrange for the client to send the string:

This was sent by the client.

and arrange for the server to send the string:

This was sent by the server.

_____ 2. Verify that your client and server work correctly.

_____ 3. Extend the server to transmit data from a file instead of a short string. For example, accept a file name as a command-line argument, and transmit the entire file. Once the file has been sent, use shutdown to terminate further transmission, and then read and display the string from the client.

_____ 4. Modify the client to also transmit data from a file, and test the client and server when sending files of various sizes. Which of the following sizes work: 32 bytes, 1K bytes, 10K bytes, and 100K bytes?

Optional Extensions (checkmark options as they are completed)

_____ 5. Explain the behavior experienced with large files.

Notes

9

Experiments With Protocols From The TCP/IP Suite

9.1 Introduction

Unlike previous chapters, the experiments in this chapter focus on standard TCP/IP protocols. Furthermore, the experiments all suggest testing against live servers in the Internet. Thus, instead of asking an experimenter to design a new protocol, the experiments require the experimenter to build software that interoperates with production Internet systems.

9.2 Difficulties And Rewards

Building software that can be used in the Internet is difficult for three reasons. First, an experimenter must consult standards documents to learn about the protocol or protocols. Unfortunately, such documents are not designed for beginners; they are terse and often difficult to comprehend. Second, unlike previous experiments, every detail matters. Experiments in previous chapters ask an experimenter to build both sides of a communication system. As long as both sides agree, they can work even if the experimenter omits features, simplifies the design, or violates the written specification. However, before a program can interact with a standard protocol system, the implementation must be both correct and complete. Third, using a production system to debug protocol software is difficult because such systems are not usually designed to assist in debugging. When it receives an incorrect or unexpected message, a production system may discard the message without response or may issue a response that is impossible to decipher. In fact, a programmer may not even be able to determine whether messages have reached the intended destination. Thus, the experimenter may have little or no help in finding problems.

Despite the difficulties, building software that interacts with production facilities can be both exciting and rewarding. Interoperability is the cardinal test of internetworking software — it verifies that the experimenter understood the protocol specification and built software to implement it correctly. An experimenter often feels extra satisfaction and pride when their software successfully interacts with a production system.

9.3 Summary

This chapter focuses on standard protocols. Reading standards documents and testing against production servers is more difficult than designing software for both ends of a protocol. Because interoperability is an essential aspect of protocol software, learning to build programs that interoperate with production systems is rewarding.

Experiment 9.1
Build A Client For The TIME Protocol

Purpose

To learn how the Internet represents the time of day and how the Time protocol works.

Background Reading And Preparation

Read RFC 868, which defines the Time protocol.

Overview

Build an application program that obtains the time from a server and prints the current date and time in a form suitable for someone to read.

Procedure And Details (checkmark as each is completed)

_____ 1. Write an application that becomes a client of an Internet Time server. Have the application accept the name of a computer on which the server runs as an argument. Following the protocol specification, send a UDP message to the server (protocol port 37), obtain a response, and print the response in hexadecimal.

_____ 2. Test the program by sending a message to a computer on the Internet that is known to run a Time server.

_____ 3. The Internet represents time as a 32-bit integer that gives the number of seconds past January 1, 1900, UCT†. However, the integer is stored in *network byte order*, which may differ from the byte order on the local computer. Rewrite the program to convert the date from network byte order to local byte order (e.g., using function *ntohl*), and display the result in a printable form such as:

7:30 PM Thursday, June 12, 2003

---

†UCT was formerly called *Greenwich Mean Time*.

Optional Extensions (checkmark options as they are completed)

_____ 4. Extend the program to accept an optional argument that specifies the time zone (either as a string or as a number of hours from UCT) and adjust the time to the local time zone.

_____ 5. Build the program to try contacting the server via UDP, and then, if no response is received within 3 seconds, to try contacting the server via TCP.

Notes

Experiment 9.2
Build A DNS Client Program

Purpose

To learn how to build a client for the Domain Name System.

Background Reading And Preparation

For an overview of the Domain Name System (DNS), read Chapter 31 in *Computer Networks And Internets*. The exact specifications of the protocol can be found in RFCs 1034 and 1035, which have been updated by RFC 2181. Although the specifications are both long and tedious, it will be necessary to consult them. The file *domain.h* that defines the format of DNS messages using C declarations can be found in directory:

ftp.cs.purdue.edu/pub/comer/labbook/lab9.2

A packet capture tool will also be useful in debugging. Later experiments ask you to construct such a tool. If you have not built a tool yourself, look at Experiment 3.5, which specifies downloading a shareware tool.

Overview

Build a DNS client that looks up a domain name and displays the corresponding IP address.

Procedure And Details (checkmark as each is completed)

_____ 1. Build a client program that uses UDP to send a query message containing one question to a DNS server on port 53. The message consists of the ten items listed below. All integer values in the message must be represented in network byte order (use function *htons* or an equivalent).

Field	Type	Value
ID	16-bit integer	any value
Parameter	16-bit integer	0x100
Question count	16-bit integer	1
Answer count	16-bit integer	0
Authority count	16-bit integer	0
Add. info count	16-bit integer	0
Length	8 bit integer	L
Domain name	L bytes	ASCII characters of name
Lookup type	16-bit integer	1
Lookup class	16-bit integer	1

_____ 2. To test the client, look up the name *www.netbook.cs.purdue.edu* and dump the response in hexadecimal.

_____ 3. Augment the program to print the IP address from the response in dotted decimal.

_____ 4. Test the client by looking up a set of well-known domain names and verifying that the server returns the correct IP address for each.

Optional Extensions (checkmark options as they are completed)

_____ 5. Extend the DNS client to handle DNS mail exchanger lookups (type *MX* records).

_____ 6. Read about using DNS pointer queries (i.e., looking up an IP address to obtain a domain name), and extend the DNS client to provide pointer query lookup.

Experiment 9.3
Build A DHCP Client

Purpose

To learn how computers use the DHCP protocol to bootstrap and how to build a DHCP client program.

Background Reading And Preparation

Read Chapter 41 in *Computer Networks And Internets* to learn about the DHCP protocol and the DHCP message format. Consult RFCs 2131 and 2132 for further details about the protocol.

A packet capture tool will also be useful in debugging. Later experiments ask you to construct such a tool. If you have not built a tool yourself, look at Experiment 3.5, which specifies downloading a shareware tool.

Overview

Implement and test a DHCP client program.

Procedure And Details (checkmark as each is completed)

_____ 1. Build a program that forms a DHCP *discover* message. Begin by setting the entire message to zero and then filling in specific fields as needed. For example, set the operation field to specify a discover message (value *1*), set the hardware type for the local network (Ethernet has hardware type *1* and address length *6*). The leftmost bit of the FLAGS field must be set for a broadcast request.

_____ 2. Test the program by broadcasting the message (e.g., broadcast the message to port 67 on the local network), and dumping the reply in hexadecimal.

_____ 3. Revise the program to display fields from the reply message in a readable format.

_____ 4. Test the program by sending a query and displaying the results.

Optional Extensions (checkmark options as they are completed)

_____ 5. Extend the program to send a DHCP *request* message. Specify a DHCP option at the end of the message that consists of the following four octets:

Description	value
DHCP code	53
Length	1
Type	3
End	255

_____ 6. Read about DHCP leases. Extend the program to obtain an address with a specified lease time.

_____ 7. Extend your application to use TFTP to obtain a copy of the boot file that is specified in the DHCP response, and verify that the program obtains the correct file.

Notes

Part III
Network Measurement And Packet Analysis Experiments On Augmented, Shared Workstation Labs

Measurement Of Throughput And Analysis Of Protocols That Can Be Carried Out Using A Lab Augmented With A Small Amount Of Additional Network Hardware

10

Hardware And Software For An Augmented Shared Lab

10.1 The Ideal Measurement Lab

An ideal lab for measurement and packet analysis consists of a completely isolated Local Area Network plus a set of computers over which the experimenter has absolute control. Isolation guarantees that the network can be used for measurements without interference (i.e., no unexpected packets travel across the lab network during a measurement). Control means that an experimenter can repeat each experiment many times using exactly the same environment in each instance. The combination increases accuracy of measurements.

Although it is possible to perform measurements and packet analysis using only two computers, an ideal lab has at least three. A third computer allows an experimenter to measure protocols without impacting the system being measured. That is, two of the computers can run a standard (i.e., unmodified) operating system, conventional protocol software, and conventional client-server applications. The third computer can be programmed to capture or monitor packets passively, without affecting the two communicating systems.

10.2 Alternatives To An Isolated Network

Although it provides the ideal environment for measurement, an isolated lab has several disadvantages. First, because the equipment is not shared, the entire cost falls to the group performing measurements. Second, an isolated lab requires additional physical space, which is often more difficult to justify than the economic cost. Third, an isolated lab imposes significant overhead because an administrator must establish accounts for users, manage disk space, and handle backups.

Fortunately, alternatives exist. Some institutions simply use computers connected to a production network. Of course, traffic on the network will affect measurements, making it difficult to ensure accuracy. Furthermore, users are not generally permitted to capture packets from a production network because the traffic includes sensitive information such as passwords as well as copies of work by others. To avoid using a production network, some academic institutions use older, slower computers that would normally be scrapped to build an isolated lab. Although such a facility works well for protocol analysis experiments, out-of-date hardware cannot produce realistic measurements. Industrial testbeds, which are often established to measure performance, tend to avoid using older hardware because it skews the measurements.

10.3 Augmentation

How can an institution achieve the benefits of an isolated network and high-speed computers without paying for equipment or devoting space to such a lab? One possibility involves augmenting workstations on a production network. An additional network interface card is added to each workstation, and the extra interfaces are connected to a private network. We say that the workstations are *dual-homed* (i.e., connected to more than one network). For example, Figure 10.1 illustrates a lab in which groups of four dual-homed workstations each have a second interface card connected to a private network.

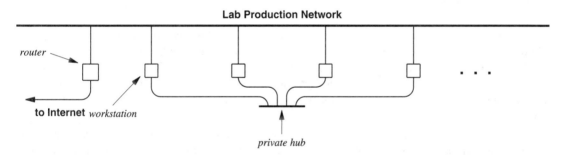

Figure 10.1 An inexpensive architecture that has many of the benefits of an isolated network. An additional interface card in each workstation connects to a private network.

10.4 Protecting The Production Network

How is it possible to allow users to capture packets on the private network without allowing them to capture packets on the production network? The answer lies in the way the operating system handles protection. Typically, network devices are protected so they can only be accessed by a user with administrative privilege (*superuser* privilege in UNIX). Thus, if an average user attempts to run an application that captures packets from a network, the application will be denied access. For example, on many systems, the *tcpdump* application is used to capture a copy of all (or selected) network packets. If an average user attempts to use tcpdump, the system will deny access, and the application will fail.

To give users access to the private network, an administrator uses the *sudo* command†. Sudo takes a complete command as an argument. That is, sudo receives the name of a command plus arguments to that command. Sudo checks the values of the arguments, and consults a configuration file to determine whether the user is allowed to run the specified command with the specified arguments. If the requested command is approved, sudo runs the command with superuser privilege. Thus, sudo can be set to allow an arbitrary user to run tcpdump on the private network, while denying users the ability to run tcpdump on the production network. The point is: protected network interfaces plus a modest amount of system configuration make it possible to prevent users from capturing packets on the production network while allowing them to capture packets on the private network.

10.5 Computers On A Private Network

How many computers should be connected to a private network? The answer depends on the experiments to be run. For example, as we described above, having at least three computers on the network makes it easy to analyze protocols: one computer captures all the packets, while the other two computers communicate (e.g., transfer a file). Having four computers makes it possible to measure the effect of traffic. For example, it is possible to compare the speed of a file transfer from computer A to computer B under two conditions: the network contains no other traffic, or the network is used for a simultaneous transfer from computer C to computer D. Of course, if the lab contains N workstations, connecting four of them to each private network results in at most $N/4$ private networks. Thus, if fewer workstations are connected to each private network, more experimenters can use the lab simultaneously.

10.6 Summary

An ideal facility for network measurement and packet capture experiments consists of an isolated network and a set of computers over which the experimenter has absolute control. The chief disadvantages of an isolated network arise from the cost of the equipment and the requirement for physical space. Several alternative architectures exist; each has some advantages.

One alternative to an isolated network consists of augmenting a shared, production lab. Each workstation in the lab is given an extra interface card, and the extra cards are used to connect the workstation to a private network. Operating system protection and software such as *sudo* prevent users from capturing packets on the production network, while allowing them to capture packets on the private network.

---

†In version 8 of Solaris, a similar facility is known as *rbac*.

11

Network Measurement Experiments

11.1 Introduction

Experiments in earlier chapters concentrate on building new applications that communicate over an internet or devising new protocols to solve communication problems. This chapter and others in this section take a different approach. They assume an internet is in place, and focus on studying its performance. Experiments in this chapter explore performance of the underlying network hardware. Later chapters focus on the operation of protocol software at various layers.

11.2 Measuring Throughput

Network architects use *throughput* as the primary measure when planning a communication system. The throughput of a given piece of hardware determines its capacity, and the hardware with the least throughput can be a bottleneck. Thus, it is important to be able to measure and understand throughput.

Experiments in this chapter assess the throughput of the underlying hardware by sending data across the hardware and measuring the rate. We begin by exploring software used to analyze throughput. The experimenter is then asked to compare the throughput of two different hardware devices and to compare the throughput of a network with and without additional load.

To measure throughput, we use a tool that is both widely available and extremely popular: a client-server application known as *ttcp*†. The acronym stands for *Test TCP*, a name that was originally chosen because the software measures the rate at which data can be transferred from one computer to another using the TCP protocol. Modern computer hardware and protocol software work so well, however, that ttcp can be used to assess throughput of the underlying network.

---

†The ttcp program described here should not be confused with the ToolTalk file copy command available on the Solaris operating system which also uses the name ttcp.

11.3 Summary

To investigate and compare the capacity of the underlying network hardware, we will measure throughput of data sent between computers on the network.

Experiment 11.1
Compile And Test ttcp

Purpose

To obtain a copy of ttcp software and learn how to use it

Background Reading And Preparation

Information on the ttcp program can be found on many web sites; a web search will produce several references.

Overview

Obtain, compile, and run a copy of ttcp software to measure throughput.

Procedure And Details (checkmark as each is completed)

_____ 1. Obtain a copy of ttcp. Web sites exist that contain public domain copies of source or binary versions of the program for various operating systems†. Source code suitable for UNIX systems can be obtained from:

ftp.cs.purdue.edu/pub/comer/labbook/ttcp.c

_____ 2. Compile ttcp to obtain a binary. Note: you may need to link the binary with the socket library.

_____ 3. Test ttcp in loopback on a single computer: start one copy in receive mode and another copy in transmit mode with a large file as input (i.e., at least a megabyte). For the UNIX version, the command lines needed are:

```
ttcp -r > /dev/null
ttcp -t localhost < largefile
```

---

†Note: Cisco routers include ttcp as an undocumented command. Enter *ttcp* on the IOS console to determine if your router includes it.

_____ 4. Ttcp reports the size of data sent (in bytes) and the time taken. From the ttcp output, compute and record the loopback throughput to three significant digits (in Kbps):

_____

_____ 5. Repeat the loopback test using UDP (the -*u* option for the UNIX version of ttcp), and compute and record the throughput to three significant digits (in Kbps):

_____

_____ 6. Using TCP to obtain measurements, plot the throughput for buffer sizes ranging from 16K bytes to 256K in increments of 16K. (Note: the -*b* option is used to specify buffer size in the UNIX version of ttcp.)

Optional Extensions (checkmark options as they are completed)

_____ 7. The -*T* option causes the sending ttcp to "touch" each byte of data as it is written (i.e., to emulate processing). Repeat the TCP measurement with the -*T* option set. How much is throughput affected?

_____ 8. Repeat the TCP measurements with various size files. Does throughput vary with file size?

_____ 9. Repeat the TCP measurements with output from the receiving ttcp directed to a file instead of */dev/null*. How much is throughput affected?

Notes

Experiment 11.2
Measure 10 and 100 Mbps Network Throughput

Purpose

To learn how to measure network throughput and compare the end-to-end throughput achieved when the underlying network capacity differs.

Background Reading And Preparation

Read Chapter *15* in *Computer Networks And Internets* to learn about *throughput* as a measure of network performance. Information on the ttcp program can be found on many web sites; a web search will produce several references.

Overview

Use ttcp to measure throughput across a 10 Mbps network and a 100 Mbps network.

Procedure And Details (checkmark as each is completed)

_____ 1. Obtain ttcp software and configure it to use the private network between two workstations. If using a lab that has both a production network and a private network, specify the domain name or IP address assigned to the destination computer's private interface. To verify that data is passing across the private network, temporarily disconnect the private network (e.g., for 30 seconds) during a transfer to see if the transfer time increases.

_____ 2. Using a 100 Mbps network hub as the private network, conduct a sequence of ten measurements using ttcp with a file size of five megabytes. Ensure that the workstations are otherwise idle and that no other traffic is being sent across the private network during the experiment.

_____ 3. For the 100 Mbps network, compute and record three values.

The mean throughput in Kbps:

_____

the standard deviation:

_____

the percentage of the underlying network that was occupied by data:

_____

_____ 4. Replace the 100 Mbps hub with a 10 Mbps hub, and repeat Step 2.

_____ 5. For the 10 Mbps network, compute and record three values.

The mean throughput in Kbps:

_____

the standard deviation:

_____

the percentage of the underlying network that was occupied by data:

_____

Optional Extensions (checkmark options as they are completed)

_____ 6. Repeat the 100 Mbps and 10 Mbps measurements using UDP. By how much does the throughput differ?

_____ 7. If the underlying network is an Ethernet and each data frame contains 1500 octets of data, how many frames would be sent to transfer an entire five megabyte file?

Experiment 11.3
Compare Throughput Of A Switch And A Hub

Purpose

To learn about the performance of a switch and a hub.

Background Reading And Preparation

Read Chapter 11 in *Computer Networks And Internets* to learn about the conceptual differences between a hub and a switch. Information on the ttcp program can be found on many web sites; a web search will produce several references.

Overview

Use ttcp to measure throughput across a hub and switch with and without cross traffic.

Procedure And Details (checkmark as each is completed)

_____ 1. *Switch without cross-traffic.* Install a switch as the private network connecting a pair of workstations, and use ttcp to measure throughput (ensure the workstations are otherwise idle and that no other traffic is present on the private network). Take multiple measurements of a large file transfer; compute and record the mean throughput:

_____

_____ 2. *Switch with cross-traffic.* Repeat the measurements in the presence of cross-traffic. Add two other computers to the private network and arrange for them to send data continuously while repeating the test. Compute and record the mean throughput of multiple runs with cross-traffic:

_____

_____ 3. *Hub with cross-traffic.* Replace the switch with a hub and repeat the measurements using two additional computers to generate cross-traffic. Compute and record the mean throughput of multiple runs:

_____

_____ 4. *Hub without cross-traffic.* Stop the cross-traffic, and disconnect the two extra computers from the hub. Repeat the measurements; compute and record the mean throughput of multiple runs:

_____

Optional Extensions (checkmark options as they are completed)

_____ 5. Repeat the measurements of throughput with a switch when the cross-traffic consists of broadcast or multicast traffic (e.g., write an application to multicast UDP datagrams). Compare the throughput to the case where cross-traffic is unicast.

_____ 6. If the switch and hub hardware is available for both 10 and 100 Mbps data rates, repeat the measurements for both data rates. Compute and record the amount by which cross traffic affects performance at each data rate.

_____

_____ 7. Extend the measurements of hub performance by adding additional cross-traffic (i.e., additional pairs of computers). Plot the throughput with no additional traffic, additional traffic from one pair of computers, additional traffic from two pairs, and so on.

12

Packet Capture And Analysis Experiments

12.1 Introduction

Capturing and analyzing packets from a live network is the best way to understand the format of packets that protocols send. Experiments in this chapter focus on packet analysis. That is, they treat each packet in isolation — once a packet has been captured, it is decoded and analyzed without knowing about previous or successive packets. Experiments in the next chapter extend the analysis to handle sequences of packets.

12.2 Promiscuous Mode And Hubs

Packet capture experiments are possible because the hardware is readily available. In fact, most Local Area Network interface cards support a facility known as *promiscuous mode* that device driver software can control. Once a device driver sets promiscuous mode reception, the card delivers a copy of every frame that crosses the network.

Of course, promiscuous mode reception only works with a hub. A computer cannot capture arbitrary packets from a switch because the switch hardware does not pass copies of all packets to all ports. Thus, for all packet capture experiments we assume a hub is used.

12.3 Manual Packet Inspection

The experiments in this chapter each suggest creating a computer program to analyze packets that have been captured. Writing a packet analysis program requires low-level programming skills, including knowing how to extract items from a header, convert integers to local byte order, and manipulate bit fields. Typically, the programming is done using the C programming language.

Experimenters who do not have the necessary programming background can still perform analysis manually. To do so, the experimenter begins by printing the packet contents in hexadecimal (at least double spaced to make the output easy to read). The experimenter then marks off each item in the packet header, and manually converts values to an appropriate form. Interestingly, programmers can also employ manual packet inspection to verify that their software is working correctly.

12.4 Summary

Experiments in this chapter focus on the analysis of individual packets that are captured from a live network; the next chapter extends the analysis to sequences of packets. Experimenters who do not have a background in low-level programming can benefit from performing manual packet analysis.

Experiment 12.1
Capture And Decode Ethernet Frames

Purpose

To learn how to capture frames from a live network and analyze their contents.

Background Reading And Preparation

Read about the Ethernet frame format in Chapter 9 of *Computer Networks And Internets*. Consult your local computer system for information about *tcpdump* or a similar program that can capture packets from a live network. You can also find general information and source code for *tcpdump* at:

http://ee.lbl.gov/

Overview

Run an application that captures one or more frames from a private network and places them in a file; write an application that analyzes the resulting data.

Procedure And Details (checkmark as each is completed)

_____ 1. Connect three computers to a private network. On one computer run *tcpdump* (or an equivalent program such as *snoop* or *etherfind*) to capture frames from the private network and place them in a file. Arrange for the other two computers to generate traffic by having them use *ping* or another application that uses the network.

_____ 2. Write an application that reads the captured frames from a file and displays the header fields (48 bit destination address, 48 bit source address, and 16-bit type field) in hexadecimal.

_____ 3. Instead of displaying the Ethernet type field in hexadecimal, extend the program to print a short name for the types you encounter. A list of Ethernet types and frame details can be found in:

http://www.iana.org/assignments/ethernet-numbers

_____ 4. Modify your program to indicate frames that contain broadcast or multicast addresses.

Optional Extensions (checkmark options as they are completed)

_____ 5. Extend your application to display a prefix of the frame data area in both hexadecimal and as characters (map each nonprintable character to an asterisk).

_____ 6. Find the Ethernet addresses of computers in your lab, and arrange for your program to convert the addresses to names of computers.

Notes

Experiment 12.2
Decode An IP Header

Purpose

To learn how to decode header fields in an IP datagram.

Background Reading And Preparation

Read Chapter 20 in *Computer Networks And Internets* to learn about the IP datagram format and header fields. Read Chapter 7 in *Internetworking With TCP/IP Volume 1: Principles, Protocols, And Architecture* or RFC 791 for further details about the IP header.

Overview

Capture one or more frames that carry an IP datagram. Extract and display the fields in the IP datagram header.

Procedure And Details (checkmark as each is completed)

_____ 1. Use *tcpdump* or a similar program to capture frames. Specify that the program should capture frames carrying IP datagrams.

_____ 2. Write an application to extract fields of an IP datagram header and display them in hexadecimal. The application should begin by verifying that the type field in the Ethernet frame contains the IP type (value 0x0800). It should then extract and display each field by giving the name of the field and the contents.

_____ 3. Modify the application to display the IP source and destination addresses in dotted decimal format.

_____ 4. Modify the application to display each integer header field as a decimal value. Use *ntohs* or an equivalent function to convert the field from network byte order to the local byte order.

_____ 5. Modify the application to identify individual bits of the *FLAGS* field.

_____ 6. Modify the application to display the name of the protocol that was used to create the payload (e.g., *TCP* or *ICMP*).

_____ 7. Compute and display the size of the payload carried in the datagram.

Optional Extensions (checkmark options as they are completed)

_____ 8. Extend the application by adding a table of computer names and IP addresses; instead of printing addresses in dotted decimal, look up and print the computer's name.

_____ 9. Extend the application to display the beginning of the payload area. Arrange to print one line in a ''dump'' format that has hexadecimal values for the first 20 octets of the payload followed by the 20 characters that give the printable version of the octets. If a given octet is not printable, display a period instead.

_____ 10. Extend the application to convert an arbitrary IP address to an equivalent name — use a DNS pointer query lookup to perform the translation.

_____ 11. Read about IP options, and extend the application to decode values from the options field if any options are present.

Notes

Experiment 12.3
Decode TCP Segment Headers

Purpose

To learn how to decode header fields in a TCP segment.

Background Reading And Preparation

Read Chapter 25 in *Computer Networks And Internets* to learn about fields in a TCP segment and how a segment is encapsulated in a datagram. Read Chapter 13 in *Internetworking With TCP/IP Volume 1: Principles, Protocols, And Architecture* or RFC 793 for further details about fields in the TCP segment.

Overview

Capture one or more frames that carry an IP datagram with a TCP segment encapsulated in the datagram. Extract and display fields of the TCP segment header.

Procedure And Details (checkmark as each is completed)

_____ 1. Use *tcpdump* or a similar program to capture frames. Specify that the program should capture datagrams carrying TCP.

_____ 2. Write an application to extract fields of the TCP segment header and display them in hexadecimal. Use the HEADER LENGTH field of the IP datagram to locate the beginning of the TCP segment. Arrange to display one line of output for each field, with each line containing the name of the field followed by the value in hexadecimal.

_____ 3. Modify the application to convert integer fields in the header to the computer's byte order and print them as decimal values. To do so, use functions *ntohs* and *ntohl* or equivalent functions.

_____ 4. Modify the application to identify individual bits of the *CODE* field.

_____ 5. Compute and display the size of the payload carried in the segment. Note: you must use the *TOTAL LENGTH* field in the IP datagram to compute the segment size.

Optional Extensions (checkmark options as they are completed)

_____ 6. Use *getservbyport* or an equivalent function to translate numbers found in the *SOURCE PORT* and *DESTINATION PORT* fields to service names.

_____ 7. Extend the application to display the beginning of the data carried in the segment. Arrange to print one line in a ''dump'' format that has hexadecimal values for the first 20 octets of the payload followed by the 20 characters that give the printable version of the octets. If a given octet is not printable, display a period instead.

_____ 8. Read about the *URGENT* code bit and pointer. Modify the application so it prints an additional line of output containing the first octet of urgent data if the *URGENT* code bit is set.

_____ 9. Read about segment options, and decode options that are present in the segment.

Notes

Experiment 12.4
Build A Packet Analyzer

Purpose

To learn how to build a packet analyzer.

Background Reading And Preparation

Review Ethernet, IP, and TCP headers (Chapters 9, 20 and 25 in *Computer Networks And Internets*).

Overview

Build a network analyzer application that captures packets from a network and analyzes them.

Procedure And Details (checkmark as each is completed)

_____ 1. Write an application that reads a set of packets and produces the following summaries:

> Layer 2 Summary (Ethernet)
>> Total number of frames processed
>> Average frame size (excluding header)
>> Number and percentage of broadcast frames
>> Number and percentage of multicast frames
>> Number and percentage of unicast frames
>> Number and percentage of each of top five frame types

Layer 3 Summary (IP)

Total number of datagrams processed
Average datagram size (excluding header)
Number and percentage of datagram fragments
Number and percentage of datagrams sent to network broadcast address
Number and percentage of datagrams sent to limited broadcast
Number and percentage of datagrams carrying TCP
Number and percentage of datagrams carrying UDP
Number and percentage of datagrams carrying ICMP

Layer 4 Summary (TCP)

Total number of TCP segments processed
Average segment size (excluding header)
Number and percentage of acknowledgements (no data)
Number and percentage of data segments
Number and percentage of SYN/FIN segments
Number and percentage of each of top five destination ports
Number and percentage of each of top five source ports

_____ 2. Use three computers to test the application: two to generate traffic and a third to analyze packets. Connect all three computers to a private network, and use *tcpdump* or an equivalent program to capture a large number of packets. To generate traffic, use applications such as *telnet*, *ping*, and *traceroute*.

_____ 3. Modify the application to take arguments that specify which packets to examine. For example, argument *-ip* specifies that only frames carrying IP datagrams should be analyzed. It should also be possible to limit processing to frames sent by a specified computer.

Optional Extensions (checkmark options as they are completed)

_____ 4. Extend the set of arguments to the program to allow Boolean combinations (e.g., it should be possible to limit processing to "frames carrying IP that also contain TCP, or frames carrying ARP").

_____ 5. Modify the application to work in real-time (i.e., update the display dynamically as packets are processed).

13

Protocol Observation Experiments

13.1 Introduction

Experiments in the previous chapter focus on the analysis of individual packets. Experiments in this chapter take a broader view of protocol interaction. Instead of looking at a packet in isolation, the experiments examine how a protocol sends a sequence of packets to achieve a desired effect.

13.2 Protocol Sequences At Each Layer

As the experiments in this chapter show, protocols at each layer use sequences of packets. We will see that IP can use a sequence of fragments to send a datagram, and that TCP uses a sequence of segments to send a large file. Of course, each TCP segment is encapsulated in an IP datagram, which may be fragmented. Thus, before one can capture and interpret a sequence of layer 4 packets (i.e., TCP segments), it must be possible to interpret a sequence of layer 3 packets (i.e., IP datagrams). As a result, the experiments are arranged to start with IP reassembly and then move on to TCP stream interpretation.

13.3 Summary

Instead of viewing packets in isolation, experiments in this chapter examine the sequence of packets a protocol sends. Interpreting a sequence at a given layer requires correct interpretation at lower layers.

Experiment 13.1
Capture And Reassemble IP Fragments

Purpose

To learn how to reassemble IP fragments into a complete datagram.

Background Reading And Preparation

Read Chapter 20 in *Computer Networks And Internets* for a general description of the Internet Protocol, and Chapter 21 for a description of fragmentation and reassembly. Consult RFC 791 to learn the details of IP header fields used in fragmentation, and RFC 815 for information about reassembly.

Overview

Construct and test an application program that reassembles fragments to produce a datagram.

Procedure And Details (checkmark as each is completed)

_____ 1. Write an application that scans a list of frames, selects the first fragment encountered in the list, and reassembles the complete datagram. Allow for a maximum size datagram (64K octets). Note that fragments have the same header as a standard datagram, but the *FRAGMENT* bit is set in the *FLAGS* field. Also note that the *MORE FRAGMENTS* bit specifies whether a fragment is from the tail of the original datagram. Finally, the *FRAGMENT OFFSET* field, which specifies where the data in the fragment belongs in the original datagram, must be multipled by 8 to convert it to a byte offset. To determine when all fragments have arrived, maintain a list of fragments with the offset and size of each.

_____ 2. Test your application. To do so, connect three computers on a private network. Run *tcpdump* or a similar application to capture packets on one computer, and use the other two computers to generate traffic. To force fragmentation, run the *ping* program with a data size larger than the network MTU (e.g., on an Ethernet, specify a data size greater than 1500). Verify that the reassembled datagram contains sensible data (it is easy to tell because the data generated by most implementations of ping consists of octets with sequentially increasing values).

_____ 3. Extend your application to handle fragment loss and out-of-order delivery.

_____ 4. Stress test your extended application either by using an emulation gateway to randomly drop and reorder packets or by writing an application that randomly reorders the list of captured packets before your application processes them.

Optional Extensions (checkmark options as they are completed)

_____ 5. Extend the application so it can reassemble multiple datagrams at the same time, and devise a stress test that sends your application a mixture of fragments from multiple datagrams.

_____ 6. Optimize your application to keep the linked list of fragments for a given datagram in the same buffer used to hold the reassembled datagram.

Notes

Experiment 13.2
Extract Data From A TCP Stream

Purpose

To learn how the Transmission Control Protocol (TCP) sends a data stream and how to extract the stream from a sequence of TCP segments.

Background Reading And Preparation

Read Chapter 25 in *Computer Networks And Internets* for a general description of TCP and information about the segment format. Read RFC 793 for more details about TCP.

Overview

Build and test an application that captures a sequence of frames carrying TCP segments (each encapsulated in an IP datagram), and extracts the stream of data being transferred.

Procedure And Details (checkmark as each is completed)

_____ 1. Write an application that scans a sequence of frames and extracts a set of IP datagrams that carry data from a single TCP connection. Only examine data segments traveling in one direction. That is, watch for a *SYN* segment followed by a sequence of segments carrying data, followed by a *FIN* segment.

_____ 2. Test your application. To do so, connect three computers on a private network. Run *tcpdump* or a similar application to capture packets on one computer, and use *ttcp* on the other two computers to transfer a file.

_____ 3. Extend your application to handle packet errors (e.g., retransmitted segments, segments that arrive out-of-order, or a sequence that does not terminate with a *FIN*). Use TCP sequence numbers to place segments in order, and keep a log of problems encountered.

_____ 4. Stress test your application to verify that it handles retransmissions correctly. To generate a retransmission, unplug the receiving computer from the private network for one second while the transfer is in progress.

_____ 5. Stress test your application to verify that it handles out-of-order packets. To emulate loss or packet reordering, write an application that rearranges captured segments before processing them.

Optional Extensions (checkmark options as they are completed)

_____ 6. Modify your program so it handles IP fragmentation (i.e., the datagram carrying a TCP segment can be fragmented), and test the result.

_____ 7. Extend your application to extract data flowing in both directions across the TCP connection.

Notes

Experiment 13.3
Observe Concurrent TCP Connections

Purpose

To learn how a concurrent web server handles multiple TCP connections at the same time.

Background Reading And Preparation

Read Chapter 25 in *Computer Networks And Internets* to learn about TCP and the TCP segment format. Read Chapter 28 to learn how clients and servers use protocol port numbers.

Overview

Build and test an application that observes the TCP streams exchanged among a set of clients and a web server.

Procedure And Details (checkmark as each is completed)

_____ 1. Write an application that scans a sequence of frames and extracts a set of IP datagrams that carry TCP segments to a web server (i.e., segments destined to port 80 on a specified IP address). Use the presence of *SYN* and *FIN* segments to indicate the beginning and end of each TCP connection. Compute the maximum number of connections that occur at any time.

_____ 2. To test your program, use at least three computers: one to run your application, one to run a web server, and one or more to generate web requests. For example, start multiple concurrent browsers, and arrange for them to request pages concurrently. Note: if you do not have administrative privilege, run the server on a non-privileged protocol port.

_____ 3. Extend your application to display a series of lines that show each time a connection forms (i.e., a *SYN* segment occurs) and each time a connection terminates (i.e., a *FIN* occurs). For each event, display four items: the source and destination IP addresses and the source and destination protocol port numbers.

_____ 4. Test your program using the experimental setup described in Step 2.

Optional Extensions (checkmark options as they are completed)

_____ 5. Extend your program to analyze each TCP connection and record all data sent to the server. Establish a separate log file for each TCP connection. Test your program by arranging for browsers to send HTTP requests for well-known URLs.

_____ 6. Extend your program to capture and record data sent in the reverse direction (i.e., data the server sends back across the TCP connection to the browser). Test the application by using a browser to send requests to the server. Verify that the captured data corresponds to valid HTTP sessions.

Notes

Part IV
Configuration Experiments
In A Dedicated Intranet Lab

Network Configuration Experiments
That Can Be Carried Out In A
Completely Dedicated Intranet

14

Hardware And Software For A Dedicated Intranet Lab

Previous sections of the text explore experiments that can be performed using conventional computers attached to a conventional network. In particular, they assume that the infrastructure remains intact during the experiments. This section begins a discussion of experiments on the infrastructure itself — experiments that change topology, addressing, routing, and forwarding. We will see that such experiments require significant resources (i.e., multiple computers and routers).

14.1 Dedicated Vs. Production Facilities

Learning about Internet configuration requires a separate, dedicated lab facility because it requires fundamental changes that disrupt production service. For example, the best way to learn about the subtleties of Internet address assignment consists of assigning a set of addresses to hosts and routers, and then testing to verify that the resulting assignment is valid. Of course, such an experiment requires both complete control and coordination — all addresses must be changed at the same time.

Changing addresses is risky because a minor mistake in configuration can prevent computers from communicating or can result in illegal datagrams being sent into the Internet. The problem is exacerbated because address changes take time to enter, and may require rebooting computers before the addresses become effective. Thus, it may not be possible to restore a working environment quickly if an error does occur. The consequence should be clear: administrators of production systems do not allow users to change addresses. Instead, configuration experiments can only be performed on an isolated, nonproduction intranet.

14.2 Characteristics Of A Dedicated Intranet Lab

The facilities needed for configuration experiments differ from previous lab facilities in two significant ways. First, instead of many computers connected by a production network, an intranet lab consists of multiple networks plus the routers that interconnect them. Furthermore, the facilities should allow experiments that change the topology of the lab (i.e., the interconnections among networks). Second, the size of the lab depends on the experiments being conducted. To understand why the size is significant, observe that in previous labs, the size of the lab is roughly proportional to the number of groups conducting an experiment at the same time. That is, a given experiment requires only a few pieces of hardware, so the size of the lab depends on the number of experimenters. However, configuration experiments demand a minimum size facility even if only one group carries out a configuration experiment at any time. For example, it is possible to learn the mechanics of router configuration with only one router. But an experiment that assigns addresses in an intranet can only be conducted in a lab that contains multiple networks with computers attached to each network. In short, to have sufficient facilities for realistic configuration experiments, a lab must resemble a small campus intranet.

14.3 Example Equipment In A Dedicated Lab

We have asserted that a dedicated lab should resemble a small campus intranet. The first question that arises concerns size: exactly how large is a "small" campus intranet? At the extreme, an intranet needs only two networks interconnected by a router, with a host computer on each network. Unfortunately, a minimum intranet does not support reasonable experiments. For example, with one router, only one topology is possible; such a topology does not support experimentation with route propagation. With only one host computer per network, it is impossible to test alternative address assignments or to verify that an assignment scheme scales to handle multiple computers. We conclude that although one can use a minimalistic intranet to start exploring internet addressing and learn the mechanics of address configuration, it is impossible to understand more than the basics. To be useful for addressing and routing experiments, an intranet lab should contain at least five networks interconnected by at least four routers.

In addition to size, a dedicated intranet lab requires a variety of hardware and software not usually found on a typical computer. For example, many of the experiments require access to an IP router. One experiment requires an inexpensive *Network Address Translation (NAT)* device. Experiments in the chapter on web technologies require access to a special-purpose hardware device known as a *load balancer*. Finally, many experiments require special software, including routing protocol support (e.g., for RIP and OSPF), a security firewall, and software for a virtual private network facility.

Figure 14.1 contains an example of the hardware and software needed to make a dedicated intranet lab sufficient for all the experiments in this section. Of course, additional facilities that make the lab more closely resemble a campus intranet will enable larger scale experiments.

Quantity	Description Of Hardware
5	Layer 2 switches (e.g., Ethernet)
4	IP routers (preferably one with three ports)
15	PCs to use as host computers
1	Load balancer for web traffic
2	Network Address Translation boxes

Description Of Software
Routing Information Protocol (RIP)
Open Shortest Path First (OSPF)
SNMP manager station or equivalent
Web cache
Virtual Private Network (VPN)

Figure 14.1 An example of the hardware and software for a dedicated intranet lab. Additional facilities will enable more sophisticated experiments.

14.4 Summary

Because they change the network infrastructure (topology, naming, addressing, and routing), experiments in this section cannot be conducted over a production network. Instead, a dedicated intranet is needed. More important, a single experiment usually requires access to many pieces of hardware (e.g., hosts and routers).

15

Internet Address Configuration Experiments

15.1 Introduction

Experiments in previous sections focus on building application programs that communicate across an Internet and on assessing network performance. Experiments in this section take a different approach, and focus on the configuration of an internet.

15.2 Organization Of Chapters

We begin by exploring the configuration of Internet addressing. The experiments in this chapter require the experimenter to assign addresses, configure addresses in both hosts and routers, and test the resulting assignment. Experiments in later chapters expand the notion of Internet configuration by considering the configuration of web servers, load balancers, routing protocols, and protected environments.

Experiments in this chapter form a sequence. In particular, the first experiment focuses on the mechanics of address assignment (which will be needed in later experiments) rather than on the choice of addresses. Thus, the experiment uses a straightforward classful assignment with all address values given explicitly. Later experiments assume that the experimenter has mastered the mechanics of address configuration, and focus on the subtleties of choosing subnet and CIDR addresses.

15.3 Summary

Experiments in this chapter focus on the assignment of Internet addresses and the configuration of those addresses in hosts and routers.

Experiment 15.1
Configure IP Addresses

Purpose

To learn how to configure IP addresses in hosts and routers.

Background Reading And Preparation

Read about IP addresses in Chapter 18 in *Computer Networks And Internets*. To learn how to configure IP addresses in hosts and routers, consult the vendors' documentation.

Overview

Create an internet that consists of two networks interconnected by a router, and assign IP addresses to all the hosts and the router.

Procedure And Details (checkmark as each is completed)

_____ 1. Use two layer 2 switches (or hubs), an IP router, and six general purpose computers (e.g., PCs) to form an intranet as Figure 15.1 illustrates (i.e., place three host computers on each of two networks).

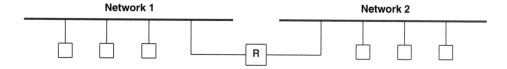

Figure 15.1 An intranet that consists of two networks with three hosts on each.

_____ 2. Use the following addresses for the two networks:

        Network 1 address: 10.0.0.0   **Address mask: 255.0.0.0**
        Network 2 address: 192.168.0.0   **Address mask: 255.255.0.0**

    Configure router R to have addresses 10.0.0.100 and 192.168.0.100.

_____ 3. Configure hosts on network 1 to have addresses: 10.0.0.1, 10.0.0.2, and 10.0.0.3 (do *not* use automatic address assignment).

_____ 4. Configure hosts on network 2 to have addresses: 192.168.0.11, 192.168.0.12, and 192.168.0.13 (do *not* use automatic address assignment).

_____ 5. Use *ping* to verify that a host on network 1 can reach either of the two router addresses as well as all other hosts.

_____ 6. Use *ping* to verify that a host on network 2 can reach either of the two router addresses as well as all other hosts.

Optional Extensions (checkmark options as they are completed)

_____ 7. Configure hosts on network 2 to use the same host suffixes as hosts on network 1 (i.e., addresses 192.168.0.1, 192.168.0.2, and 192.168.0.3), and verify that no ambiguity results.

_____ 8. Configure the router to run a DHCP server, configure the hosts to use automatic address assignment (i.e., use DHCP to obtain an address when they boot), and test the results.

Experiment 15.2
Assign Fixed-Length IP Subnet Addresses

Purpose

To learn how to assign fixed-length IP subnet addresses to an intranet.

Background Reading And Preparation

Read about IP subnet addresses in Chapter 18 in *Computer Networks And Internets*.

Overview

Create an internet that consists of five networks interconnected by four routers, and assign IP subnet addresses to the hosts and the router.

Procedure And Details (checkmark as each is completed)

_____ 1. The IP address 192.168.0.0 has two octets of network prefix and two octets of network suffix (i.e., the address mask is 255.255.0.0). Compute and record the address mask in dotted decimal if the third octet is used for subnet addressing:

255.255.255.0

_____ 2. Use five layer 2 switches (or hubs), four IP routers, and ten general purpose computers (e.g., PCs) to form the intranet topology that Figure 15.2 illustrates.

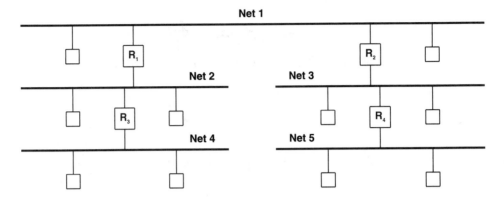

Figure 15.2 An intranet that consists of five networks connected by four IP routers.

_____ 3. Use the third octet as a subnet octet and assign a unique subnet address to each of the five
networks in your intranet. Write down the subnet addresses in dotted decimal:

Network 1 _255-255-255.1_

Network 2 _.2_

Network 3 _.3_

Network 4 _.4_

Network 5 _, 5_

_____ 4. Assign an IP address to each router interface, and configure each router with an address
and mask for each of its interfaces.

_____ 5. Configure the routing table in each router with next-hop information for each of the five
possible destination networks. (Do not enable automatic routing update protocols.)

_____ 6. Assign each host in your intranet an IP address, and configure each host to know its address. Do not use automatic address assignment.

_____ 7. Use _ping_ to test that your address assignment and configuration works correctly. Ping a
host on the same network and a host on each of the other networks.

Optional Extensions (checkmark options as they are completed)

_____ 8. Compute and record the total set of host addresses available on each network:

Net	Lowest Address	Highest Address
1		
2		
3		
4		
5		

_____ 9. Redo the experiment using twelve subnet bits instead of eight.

Experiment 15.3
Assign IP Addresses Using CIDR

Purpose

To learn how to assign IP addresses to an intranet from a CIDR block.

Background Reading And Preparation

Read about CIDR addresses in Chapter 18 in *Computer Networks And Internets*.

Overview

Create an internet that consists of five networks interconnected by four routers, and assign addresses to the hosts and the router from a CIDR block.

Procedure And Details (checkmark as each is completed)

_____ 1. Consider the CIDR block 192.168.0.0/13. Compute and record the lowest address in the block in binary:

_____

_____ 2. Use five layer 2 switches (or hubs), four IP routers, and ten general purpose computers (e.g., PCs) to form the intranet topology that Figure 15.3 illustrates.

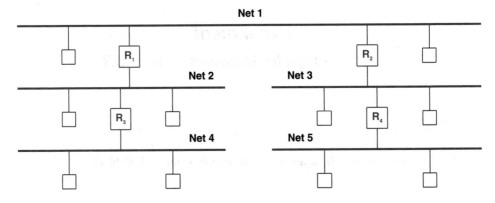

Figure 15.3 An intranet that consists of five networks connected by four IP routers.

_____ 3. Use nine additional bits (beyond the /13 prefix) for subnet addressing, and assign a unique subnet address to each of the five networks in your intranet. Write down the subnet addresses in CIDR notation:

           Network 1 _____

           Network 2 _____

           Network 3 _____

           Network 4 _____

           Network 5 _____

_____ 4. Assign an IP address to each router interface, and configure each router with an address and mask for each of its interfaces.

_____ 5. Configure the routing table in each router with next-hop information for each of the five possible destination networks. (Do not enable automatic routing update protocols.)

_____ 6. Assign each host in your intranet an IP address, and configure each host to know its address. Do not use automatic address assignment.

_____ 7. Use *ping* to test that your address assignment and configuration works correctly. Ping a host on the same network and a host on each of the other networks.

Optional Extensions (checkmark options as they are completed)

_____ 8. Compute the total set of host addresses available on each network:

Net	Lowest Address	Highest Address
1		
2		
3		
4		
5		

_____ 9. Redo the experiment assigning a /20 CIDR block to network 2, another /20 block to network 3, and two /28 blocks to networks 4 and 5.

16

Web Technology Configuration Experiments

16.1 Introduction

Experiments in the previous chapter allow one to assign and configure IP addresses in both hosts and routers. This chapter expands our exploration of configuration by exploring the technologies used in web caching.

16.2 Web Technologies

The chapter contains three experiments that each explore one of the three technologies used to create large-scale web sites: servers, load balancers, and caches. In each case, the experimenter is asked to produce a working configuration and test the result.

The next paragraphs describe two specific web technologies that are especially useful for experiments in this chapter. In each case, the technology is widely used in production web sites and is implemented by software that runs on a conventional computer. More important, the software is available for download at no cost.

Apache Web Server. The first experiment asks one to obtain and configure an Apache web server. The Apache server, which is used in many production web sites, is distributed free of charge under the GNU license. The software is available for download from the Apache Software Foundation at:

http://httpd.apache.org/

Squid Web Cache. The second experiment asks one to obtain and configure a Squid web cache. Like the Apache server, Squid is used in many production web sites, and is also distributed free of charge under the GNU license. The software is available for download from:

http://www.squid-cache.org/

16.3 Summary

Experiments in this chapter focus on the technologies used to create web sites. Two pieces of software, an Apache web server and a Squid web cache, are available for download at no charge under the GNU license.

Experiment 16.1
Configure An Apache Web Server

Purpose

To learn how to configure a web server.

Background Reading And Preparation

Read Chapter 35 in *Computer Networks And Internets* for a general description of web servers and the protocols they use. Consult the site:

http://httpd.apache.org/

for information about the Apache software and to download a copy.

Overview

Download, compile, configure, and test the Apache web server software.

Procedure And Details (checkmark as each is completed)

_____ 1. Download a copy of the source code for an Apache web server.

_____ 2. Compile the source code to create an executable binary.

_____ 3. Choose a computer, and place a set of test documents in a directory on that computer. (Note: a set of ASCII files is sufficient for testing.)

_____ 4. To test the server, choose and record a protocol port number on the computer that no other group in the lab is using (e.g., 25000, 25001, ...):

_____

_____ 5. Configure the server to map URLs into the document directory and to use the selected port number.

_____ 6. Use a browser to verify that the server works.

Optional Extensions (checkmark options as they are completed)

_____ 7. Configure the server to handle dynamic pages. For example, implement the specification of the Common Gateway Interface (CGI) at:

$$\text{http://hoohoo.ncsa.uiuc.edu/cgi/}$$

_____ 8. Test that the server is operating concurrently by having multiple clients request pages at the same time.

Notes

Experiment 16.2
Download And Configure A Squid Cache

Purpose

To learn how to configure a web cache.

Background Reading And Preparation

Read Chapter 35 in *Computer Networks And Internets* for a general description of web protocols and terminology. Consult the site:

http://www.squid-cache.org/

for information about the Squid cache software and to download a copy.

Overview

Download, compile, configure, and test the Squid web cache software.

Procedure And Details (checkmark as each is completed)

_____ 1. Download a copy of the source code for a Squid web cache.

_____ 2. Compile the source code to create an executable binary.

_____ 3. To test the server, choose and record a protocol port number on the computer that no other group in the lab is using (e.g., 31000, 31001,...):

_____

_____ 4. Configure the cache software to use the chosen port, and configure browsers on two computers to use the cache as their *proxy*.

_____ 5. To verify that documents are being retrieved from the cache, access a set of documents that have a long lifetime from one browser, disconnect the network between the cache and the origin server, and then access the documents again from the second browser.

Optional Extensions (checkmark options as they are completed)

_____ 6. Build an application that measures the difference in delay when accessing documents from an origin server and from the cache.

_____ 7. The amount of disk space devoted to the cached documents can be configured. To see how cache size affects performance, measure and plot the response time needed to repeatedly access a large set of documents for a range of cache sizes from 256K to 1G.

Notes

Experiment 16.3
Configure And Test A Web Load Balancer

Purpose

To learn how to configure a load balancer that can distribute HTTP requests among a set of web servers.

Background Reading And Preparation

Because it is new, little has been written about load balancer technology. The concept is straightforward: to handle large numbers of concurrent requests from browsers, a web site must have multiple copies of the web server running on multiple computers. A load balancer is a device that intercepts all incoming HTTP requests (i.e., requests to port 80), and sends each request to one of the servers. Thus, the servers are "hidden" behind the load balancer — the domain name of the web site maps to the IP address of the load balancer, so all browsers send their requests to the load balancer. Furthermore, each of the web servers hidden behind the load balancer operates in a standard way (i.e., receiving requests at port 80 and responding).

Details make configuration of load balancers somewhat complex. Vendors take two approaches: forwarding at layer 2 or layer 3. This experiment uses layer 3 (IP); an optional extension considers layer 2.

Overview

Create a topology with copies of web servers running on multiple computers and configure a load balancer to distribute requests among the servers.

Procedure And Details (checkmark as each is completed)

_____ 1. Use ten conventional computers to run web server software. Arrange for each computer to have an exact copy of all web pages (or use a network file system to allow all copies to share a set of files).

_____ 2. Configure a load balancer. Assuming the option is available, specify routing at layer 3. Assign the balancer an IP address, and configure it to know the IP addresses of the ten computers running web servers.

_____ 3. Use a browser to test the configuration. Specify a URL that contains the domain name (or IP address) of the load balancer, and request a page.

_____ 4. Verify that the load balancer is distributing the load among all servers. Measure which server answers a given request. If the web server is one you have written, modify the program to keep a log of requests. If the server software cannot be changed, use a packet analyzer to determine the TCP connections for each server.

Optional Extensions (checkmark options as they are completed)

_____ 5. Write an application to stress test the load balancer. Run copies of your test application on five computers, and measure the response time with one, two, three, four, and five servers.

_____ 6. If your load balancer allows it, reconfigure the balancer to use layer 2 forwarding and measure the difference in response time.

Notes

17

IP Routing And IP Forwarding Experiments

17.1 Introduction

An earlier chapter considers various forms of Internet addressing, and asks experimenters to configure values in IP forwarding tables manually†. Although manual configuration works well for the simplest topologies, most routers (and some host computers) rely on protocols that propagate routing information quickly and automatically. This chapter explores routing protocols and allows the experimenter to learn about their operation.

Routing and route propagation protocols are among the most complex topics in internetworking. The protocols are deceptive because the message format and basic operations appear to be straightforward. Unfortunately, the behavior of routing protocols is not easy to understand — many subtleties exist that can produce interesting side-effects and unexpected results. To keep the topic constrained and the experiments manageable, we avoid the more difficult aspects. All experiments use a small, straightforward internet topology. Furthermore, rather than try to explore difficult problems in routing, experiments focus on basic operations.

17.2 Indirect Vs. Direct Observation

Experiments with routing protocols fall into two broad categories: those that observe routing indirectly by using host computers to test reachability, and those that observe routing directly by examining routing tables. Indirect observation has the advantage of not requiring special tools or router access. However, indirect observations can also be ambiguous. Thus, this chapter begins by exploring the use of the *Simple Network Monitoring Protocol* (*SNMP*) which allows one to view the con-

---

†To ease configuration, some devices provide a GUI interface. For example, the device may include a web server.

tents of a routing table. As an alternative for cases where SNMP is unavailable or inconvenient, commercial routers provide console interfaces that can be used to examine or modify the routing table.

17.3 Summary

Routing is an important, but difficult subject. To prevent work from becoming unwieldy, experiments in this chapter focus on the basics.

Experiment 17.1
Use Netstat To Examine A Routing Table

Purpose

To learn how to use the Unix command *netstat* to display information from a routing table and how to understand the information.

Background Reading And Preparation

Read Chapter 20 in *Computer Networks And Internets* for an overview of IP routing. Consult the system document for information about the Unix command *netstat*.

Overview

Use netstat to view the contents of an IP routing table.

Procedure And Details (checkmark as each is completed)

_____ 1. Use the -r option of the netstat command to display the contents of an IP routing table on your local computer.

_____ 2. Go through the output from netstat and identify each field in the routing table. Make a list of IP destinations, the network mask for each, and the next hop.

_____ 3. Run netstat on a Unix router in your organization (or ask the system administrator to dump the routing table for you), and analyze each of the entries.

Optional Extensions (checkmark options as they are completed)

_____ 4. Use the -p option on netstat to examine the ARP cache from your local computer. Verify that the ARP cache is updated automatically by pinging a computer on the local network that is not present in the ARP cache.

Notes

Experiment 17.2
Use SNMP To Probe A Routing Table

Purpose

To learn how SNMP operates and to use SNMP to view the contents of a routing table.

Background Reading And Preparation

Read Chapter 39 in *Computer Networks And Internets* for a general discussion of SNMP. Consult the site:

http://net-snmp.sourceforge.net/

for information about a set of SNMP tools that can be downloaded at no charge.

Overview

Obtain a copy of an SNMP tool from the web, and use the tool to view the contents of an IP routing table.

Procedure And Details (checkmark as each is completed)

_____ 1. Download a copy of the source code for SNMP tools from the web site:

http://net-snmp.sourceforge.net/

_____ 2. Compile the source code. Be sure that the command-line programs such as *snmpget* and *snmpwalk* have been compiled into executable binaries.

_____ 3. Use the program snmpwalk to walk the MIB of a router in your intranet. You may need to know the community string that has been selected for use on computers in your lab (the string is akin to a password).

_____ 4. Access the routing table in each router in your intranet.

Optional Extensions (checkmark options as they are completed)

_____ 5. Use the tool *snmpgetnext* to fetch items from the routing table one at a time.

_____ 6. Build an application that uses SNMP to extract the contents of the routing table and format the results for display.

Notes

Name: _____

149

Experiment 17.3
Configure And Run RIP Software

Purpose

To learn how the Routing Information Protocol (RIP) works and how to configure RIP software.

Background Reading And Preparation

To learn about internet routing in general and the RIP protocol in particular, read Chapter 27 in *Computer Networks And Internets*. Further details about the RIP protocol can be found in RFC 1721. Consult the vendor's documentation for information on configuring RIP.

Overview

Create an Internet that consists of five networks interconnected by four routers, assign an IP address to each router interface, and use RIP to propagate routing information to other routers.

Procedure And Details (checkmark as each is completed)

_____ 1. Use five layer 2 switches (or hubs), four IP routers, and ten general purpose computers (e.g., PCs) to form the intranet topology that Figure 17.1 illustrates.

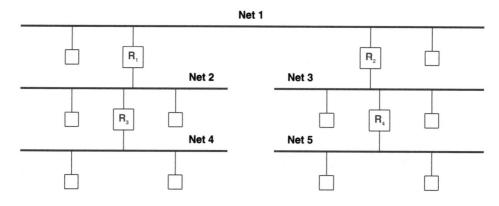

Figure 17.1 An intranet that consists of five networks connected by four IP routers.

_____ 2. Assign IP addresses to the networks:

Network	IP address	Mask
1	10.0.0.0	255.0.0.0
2	20.0.0.0	255.0.0.0
3	30.0.0.0	255.0.0.0
4	40.0.0.0	255.0.0.0
5	192.168.0.0	255.255.0.0

_____ 3. Assign a specific IP address to each router interface and each host, and configure each of the addresses. Also configure each router so that it does not run a routing protocol.

_____ 4. To verify that no routing protocols are running, wait for a few minutes, and then examine the routing tables on each router (e.g., using SNMP or the console interface). Only the local interface addresses should be present.

_____ 5. Enable RIP on each of the routers.

_____ 6. To verify that RIP has propagated routes for all five networks, wait several minutes, and examine the routing table in each router.

_____ 7. Verify that RIP detects network disconnections and changes routes automatically: break the connection between router R_2 and network 1, wait at least six minutes, and examine the routing tables again.

Optional Extensions (checkmark options as they are completed)

_____ 8. Repeat the experiment using the following subnet addresses:

Network	IP address	Mask
1	10.1.0.0	255.255.0.0
2	10.2.0.0	255.255.0.0
3	30.0.0.0	255.0.0.0
4	40.0.0.0	255.0.0.0
5	192.168.0.0	255.255.0.0

Using the routing table in router R_4, find and record the next-hop address for destination 10.1.0.0:

_____

_____ 9. Determine experimentally how long it takes RIP to converge routes. To do so, poll the routing table in a router continuously while disconnecting a network.

_____ 10. Configure one of the routers to have a default route, and verify that RIP propagates the default route throughout the intranet.

Notes

Experiment 17.4
Configure And Run OSPF Software

Purpose

To learn how the Open Shortest Path First (OSPF) protocol works and how to configure OSPF software.

Background Reading And Preparation

To learn about Internet routing in general, read Chapter 27 in *Computer Networks And Internets*. A discussion of the OSPF protocol and the specification can be found in RFC 2328. Consult the vendor's documentation for information on configuring OSPF.

Overview

Create an internet that consists of five networks interconnected by four routers, assign an IP address to each router interface, divide the intranet into two areas, and use OSPF to propagate routing information.

Procedure And Details (checkmark as each is completed)

_____ 1. Use five layer 2 switches (or hubs), four IP routers, and ten general purpose computers (e.g., PCs) to form the intranet topology that Figure 17.2 illustrates.

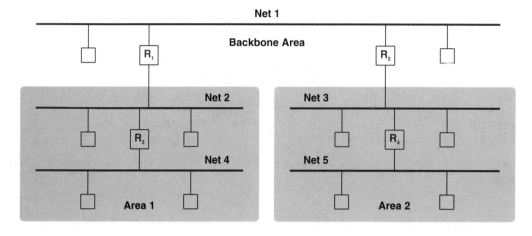

Figure 17.2 An intranet that consists of five networks connected by four IP routers. Gray shaded areas indicate groups of networks to be placed in each OSPF area.

_____ 2. Assign an IP address to each network as follows:

Network	IP address	Mask
1	10.0.0.0	255.0.0.0
2	20.0.0.0	255.0.0.0
3	30.0.0.0	255.0.0.0
4	40.0.0.0	255.0.0.0
5	192.168.0.0	255.255.0.0

_____ 3. Configure routers to run OSPF, and define three OSPF areas: a backbone and two other areas as Figure 17.2 shows. The backbone includes network 1 and routers R_1 and R_2. Note that OSPF software often expects area IDs to be entered in dotted decimal, and that the backbone has an ID of 0.0.0.0 (i.e., the value zero).

_____ 4. To verify that routers are correctly exchanging routing information, use a host on each network to ping a host on each of the other networks.

Optional Extensions (checkmark options as they are completed)

_____ 5. Expand the size of the intranet by adding more networks and routers, and repeat the experiment with additional structure inside each area.

_____ 6. To assess how fast OSPF can propagate routing information, disconnect a router and measure how long it takes OSPF to change routing tables.

Notes

18

Virtual And Protected Internet Environment Experiments

18.1 Introduction

Configuration experiments in previous chapters concentrate on the fundamentals of Internet addressing and routing. This chapter extends the set of configuration experiments to include security, virtual private networks, and address mapping. We will learn how it is possible to create internet environments that are both powerful and safe.

18.2 Flexible Abstractions

The TCP/IP technology has proven extremely flexible — the basic technology has been extended to handle security and a larger scale Internet. The flexibility arises from underlying abstractions that are effective in a variety of ways that the original designers did not foresee. Experiments in this chapter show how it is possible to use the basic abstractions to construct virtual environments that differ from the standard. Experiments will look at domain names, network address translation, and virtual private networks.

18.3 Summary

Internet technology is extremely flexible, and can be adapted to a variety of purposes. Experiments in this chapter help you learn about some of the possible extensions.

Experiment 18.1
Configure A DNS Server

Purpose

To learn how to design a naming scheme and how to configure a DNS server to implement the scheme.

Background Reading And Preparation

Read Chapter 31 in *Computer Networks And Internets* to learn about the *Domain Name System* (*DNS*). To obtain a copy of the *BIND* version of DNS software and to learn how to configure BIND, consult the *Internet Software Consortium* web site:

www.isc.org

Overview

Define an abstract namespace, obtain a copy of the BIND server software, and configure the software to implement the namespace.

Procedure And Details (checkmark as each is completed)

_____ 1. For an intranet of at least six host computers, assign IP addresses, and establish correct routes so that any computer can reach any other computer.

_____ 2. Define a new namespace for the Domain Name System. Begin with three *top-level domains* (*TLDs*): *star*, *name*, and *dot*.

_____ 3. Obtain a copy of the BIND software, compile a DNS server, and install the server on one of the host computers in your intranet.

_____ 4. Configure a DNS server to be an authority for the three new TLDs.

_____ 5. Choose a host computer, assign the computer the name *super.star* by configuring your DNS server with a mapping from *super.star* to the computer's IP address.

_____ 6. Use a tool such as *nslookup* to verify that the server maps *super.star* to the correct address.

_____ 7. Add additional entries to the name server that assign the following names to five additional computers in your intranet:

> **twinkle.little.star**
> **little.star**
> **polka.dot**
> **fourdotsfollow.dot.dot**
> **dotname.name**

_____ 8. Use a tool such as *nslookup* to verify the configuration.

Optional Extensions (checkmark options as they are completed)

_____ 9. Configure the server to support reverse DNS lookup, including the addition of a new TLD, *.arpa*. For each name, add an inverse. For example, if computer *super.star* has IP address *10.1.2.3*, define the server to have an entry:

> **3.2.1.10.in-addr.arpa**

which maps to the string *super.star*.

_____ 10. Configure your DNS server to have additional names that are aliases for existing names. Choose aliases such as:

> **www.star**
> **ftp.dot**
> **mailhub.star**
> **router.dot**
> *your-own-name*.**name**

Include at least one alias that crosses TLDs (e.g., make *ftp.dot* an alias for *super.star*).

Experiment 18.2
Install And Configure A NAT Box

Purpose

To learn how *Network Address Translation* (*NAT*) operates and how to configure NAT software.

Background Reading And Preparation

General information about Network Address Translation can be found in Chapter 20 of *Internetworking With TCP/IP Volume 1: Principles, Protocols, and Architecture.* Specific information on the Linux version of NAT (implemented with a program known as *masquerade*) can be found on the web site:

http://linas.org/linux/load.html

Overview

Establish a private intranet, configure *masquerade* to function as a NAT box, and verify that the addressing is mapped correctly.

Procedure And Details (checkmark as each is completed)

_____ 1. Use four layer 2 switches (or hubs), two IP routers, one PC running Linux (to function as a NAT box), and eight general purpose computers (e.g., PCs) to form the intranet topology that Figure 18.1 illustrates.

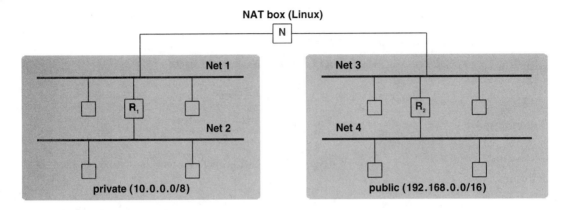

Figure 18.1 An intranet configured for NAT. The networks in one gray shaded area use private addresses; networks in the other gray shaded area can use public addresses.

_____ 2. As Figure 18.1 shows, assign addresses and configure the hosts and routers so that those on one side of the NAT box use 10.0.0.0/8 addresses to simulate a private intranet and those on the other side use 192.168.0.0/16 addresses to simulate the public Internet. When assigning addresses, also assign an address to each interface on the NAT box.

_____ 3. Configure the NAT box so it is not running any routing software.

_____ 4. Use *ping* to ensure that a computer on one side of the NAT box cannot reach a computer on the other side (i.e., verify that the NAT box is not running routing protocol software).

_____ 5. Configure the NAT box to enable address translation; treat the 10.0.0.0 addresses as private and the 192.168.0.0 addresses as public.

_____ 6. Use *ping* to verify that a host on the private side can reach a host on the public side.

Optional Extensions (checkmark options as they are completed)

_____ 7. Use a packet analyzer to capture packets that travel between the NAT box and computers on the 192.168.0.0 side, and print the source and destination addresses.

_____ 8. Run a server on a public host, and form concurrent connections to the server through the NAT box (i.e., run clients on the private side). Capture packets, and use IP addresses and protocol port numbers to associate each packet with a connection.

Notes

Experiment 18.3
Install And Configure A VPN

Purpose

To learn how to install and configure a *Virtual Private Network* (*VPN*).

Background Reading And Preparation

For a general description of Virtual Private Networks read Chapter 40 in *Computer Networks And Internets*. VPN software is available for download from the Internet at no charge. For example, the site:

http://sunsite.dk/vpnd/

offers VPN software that runs on the Linux operating system.

Overview

Create a private internet, download, install, and configure VPN software, and verify that the software encrypts all data sent between VPN locations.

Procedure And Details (checkmark as each is completed)

_____ 1. Use five layer 2 hubs, two IP routers (R_1 and R_2), two PCs running Linux (L_1 and L_2) that function as routers, and five general purpose computers (e.g., PCs) to form the intranet topology that Figure 18.2 illustrates.

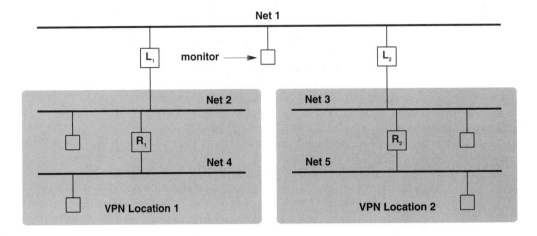

Figure 18.2 An intranet that consists of five networks. Each gray shaded area indicates a group of networks within a single VPN location.

_____ 2. Download and compile a copy of VPN software for Linux, and install the software on the two Linux boxes (labeled L_1 and L_2 in the figure).

_____ 3. Configure the VPN software to encrypt all communication that passes between the two locations.

_____ 4. To test the configuration, run software on the monitor computer that will capture and display all packets that traverse network 1. Establish communication between a computer in VPN Location 1 and a computer in VPN Location 2 (e.g., using *telnet*), and verify that the data carried in packets is not visible (i.e., all packets are encrypted).

Optional Extensions (checkmark options as they are completed)

_____ 5. Extend the configuration to three sites, and verify that the VPN correctly encrypts all communication.

_____ 6. Revise the experiment to use the global Internet as the intermediate link between two sites.

Part V
Protocol Stack Implementation
In A Special-Purpose Lab

**Protocol Stack Design And
Implementation Experiments
That Can Be Carried Out
Using A Protocol Development Lab**

19

Hardware And Software For A Special-Purpose Protocol Development Lab

19.1 Introduction

Previous chapters describe labs that support application-layer programming. The lab facilities can be assembled using off-the-shelf hardware and software. We said that in such environments, experiments with protocol design require the use of an emulation gateway. Although an emulation gateway allows one to understand general principles, experimentation is limited to basics. This chapter describes a lab that allows one to experiment with a native protocol stack. That is, instead of using an application gateway to emulate packet transmission, the lab allows us to experiment with protocol software inside an operating system kernel. The resulting protocol stack has access to network interface cards, and handles packets without depending on emulation or other protocol software. The next chapter describes experiments that can be conducted in such a lab, including the implementation of protocols needed for an IP router.

19.2 The Need For Two Computers

Production protocol software does not run as an application. The stack is either implemented as a module inside a conventional time-sharing operating system kernel, or it runs as an embedded system (e.g., in a hardwired controller). In either case, the protocol stack interacts directly with device drivers for network interface cards, and handles interrupts. Testing production protocols requires absolute privilege — the protocol software must be able to control the hardware.

In principle, a single computer provides a sufficient platform on which to develop production protocol software: the programmer first builds a new version of the system that contains modified protocol software, and then restarts the computer to run the new system. In practice, however, using a single computer is impractical. Continual rebooting requires excessive time. Furthermore, if the new system malfunctions, the programmer may be unable to use it to make changes and compile a new version. Instead, the programmer must reboot the original version of the system (which introduces a long delay).

To avoid waiting for a computer to reboot, programmers who build protocol software use two computers. One computer, called a *front-end*, provides a stable environment that is used to edit, compile, and link software. The second computer, called a *back-end*, consists of raw hardware — a back-end is an idle machine that can be rebooted at any time. A back-end does not run a standard operating system; it is only used to test a new system. When a new image has been prepared, the programmer moves the image into a back-end for testing, leaving the front-end ready to edit and compile the next version.

19.3 Front-end And Back-end Computers In A Lab

We can generalize the concept of two computers to a lab that supports multiple simultaneous users. The lab contains two types of computers: a set of conventional front-end workstations that run the editors and compilers needed to create and compile protocol software and a set of back-end computers that are available for testing.

Should a front-end and a back-end computer be configured to operate as a pair? No. There are two reasons. First, some experiments require the use of multiple back-ends. For example, to test a new (nonstandard) communication protocol, two back-end computers are needed. Second, the optimal ratio of front-ends to back-ends is determined by the way a lab is used. For example, in a typical instructional lab where students spend more time writing and compiling software than testing, a lab needs to have more front-ends than back-ends. In a production setting where extensive testing is required after a change, a lab needs more back-ends than front-ends. Thus, the architecture we describe allows arbitrary numbers of each type.

19.4 Functional Requirements

The goal is an environment that is suitable for many users to engage in protocol stack development simultaneously. To handle an arbitrary set of users and to avoid long delays, the lab must be automated. Thus, a lab architecture should include the following:

> *Arbitrary Numbers Of Front-end And Back-end Computers.* As described above, the lab should be designed to accommodate arbitrary numbers of front-end and back-end computers. In particular, the architecture should not require front-end and back-end computers to be paired. Finally, adding computers of either type should be straightforward.

Automated Back-end Allocation. A mechanism should exist that manages the set of back-ends. A user in the lab should be able to request one or more back-end computers, and the mechanism should fill the request quickly and automatically.

Fast Download. A mechanism should exist that can download a memory image from a front-end computer into a back-end computer and start the back-end running the image. To allow rapid turn-around after a change has been made, downloading and startup should take at most a few seconds.

Communication With Back-end Console. A mechanism should exist that connects a window on a user's front-end computer to the console of a back-end computer. The mechanism should provide a separate window for each back-end computer that a user allocates to allow the user to interact with the system running on the back-end (e.g., to receive debugging output).

Back-End Recovery. A mechanism should exist that provides complete control of any back-end without requiring physical access. When a user finishes with a back-end, the recovery mechanism should be able to take control of the machine. It should be possible for another user to then allocate the back-end and download a new image. The recovery mechanism should handle the worst case: a situation where a software bug causes the back-end to stop responding to console input.

19.5 An Example Architecture

To illustrate how the functional requirements relate to practical hardware and software, we will investigate the architecture of the Xinu laboratory that the author has created to teach operating systems and internetworking courses†. Figure 19.1 illustrates the Xinu lab architecture.

†The author gratefully acknowledges donations from many corporate sponsors, including Agere Systems, IBM Corporation, Intel Corporation, and many graduate students who contributed to both the facilities and the operation of the lab.

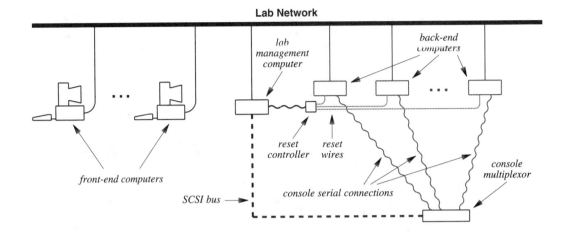

Figure 19.1 An example architecture for a lab that supports protocol stack development. Both front-end and back-end computers attach to the lab network.

Equipment in the lab can be summarized as follows.

- *Front-end Computers:* A set of workstations (e.g., PCs) running a conventional operating system (e.g., Linux).

- *Back-end Computers:* One or more CPUs that can be used for downloading (e.g., PCs).

- *Lab Management Computer:* A standard computer with a conventional operating system (e.g., a PC with Linux) that runs software used to manage, control, and download back-ends. Servers that run on the management computer include a back-end allocator, reset server, and servers to download an image. In theory, although it would be possible to run all the management software on one of the front-end computers, we use a separate CPU because significant computational resources are required for management.

- *Console Multiplexor:* a hardware device that connects multiple (RS-232) serial lines to a conventional computer over a SCSI bus. The console multiplexor, sometimes called a *terminal multiplexor* or *console access server*, allows software running on the management computer to establish communication between a window on a front-end and the console on a back-end.

- *Reset Controller:* A special-purpose hardware device, designed and built at Purdue, that provides emergency reset capability for back-ends. The reset controller has a serial connection over which it accepts commands and a set of wire pairs that each connect to the hardware "reset" switch on a back-end. If a back-end stops

responding to console commands, a user requests a reset. Software running on the
manager issues the appropriate command to the reset controller, and the reset controller emulates pressing the hardware reset switch on the back-end.

19.6 Operation Of The Author's Lab

To explain how the author's lab appears to a user, we will examine the series of steps needed
to run an image. A user begins by selecting a front-end computer and using the computer to compile the source code. The user links the compiled binary, along with supporting software (e.g.,
operating system functions and a driver for the network interface device), and places the resulting
image in a file on the front-end disk. Once the file has been created, the user invokes software that
automatically allocates a back-end, downloads the image into the back-end, and connects the user's
window to the console of the back-end so that the user can interact with the running image. Specifi-
cally, the user performs the following steps:

- *Create A Console Window (optional).* The user can create a window on the front-end for each
  back-end that will be needed. Creating a separate window per back-end is optional — if only
  one back-end is needed, any window that offers a command prompt can be used.

- *Allocate A Back-end And Connect To It.* To allocate a back-end, the user invokes the *cs-console*
  program, which becomes a client that interacts with a server which runs on the lab management
  computer. Cs-console sends a message to the server to request a back-end. Among other things,
  the message identifies the user who is running cs-console. The server finds the first available
  back-end, assigns the back-end to the user, and sends a reply informing the requesting application
  about the allocation. Cs-console then connects the user's window to the console of the back-end,
  allowing the user to send keystrokes to the back-end and receive output in the window.

  A user supplies command-line arguments to control the operation of cs-console. For example,
  one argument specifies the IP address of the server (i.e., the IP address of the lab management
  computer on which the server runs). As an alternative to command-line arguments, cs-console
  recognizes two Unix *environment variables*. Environment variable CS_SERVERS specifies the address of the computer on which the server runs, and environment variable CS_CLASS specifies the
  type of back-end needed. The latter is important in a lab that has heterogeneous back-ends because a user may need a specific type (e.g., type of CPU).

- *Escape To Command Mode.* Unless the user specifies otherwise, cs-console establishes a connection with the back-end's console and transmits all the user's keystrokes to the back-end. In particular, cs-console will forward *CONTROL-C*, the keystroke Linux uses to abort a running program. To permit a user to temporarily stop communication with the back-end, cs-console recognizes a special escape: *CONTROL-@* (ASCII null). When a user types *CONTROL-@*, cs-console
  enters *command mode*, and interacts with the user. Cs-console issues a prompt to inform the user
  that it has entered command mode, and then recognizes a set of commands that control its operation. Figure 19.2 lists the command set.

command	Meaning
h	Print a help message
?	Print a help message
b	Send a BREAK to the back-end
c	Continue session (leave command mode)
z	Suspend cs-console (like Control-Z)
d	Download image
p	Power cycle (reboot) back-end
s	Spawn a program (Linux exec)
q	Quit (cs-console exits)
Control-D	Quit (cs-console exits)

Figure 19.2 The set of commands cs-console recognizes when operating in *command mode* and the meaning of each.

- *Download The Image To The Management Computer.* Moving an image into a back-end is a two-step process. In the first step, the image is copied from the user's front-end computer to the lab management computer. In the second step, the image is copied from the management computer into the back-end. Separating the two steps makes sense because debugging often requires restarting an image multiple times — reloading is much faster once the image has been copied to the management computer.

Only a few keystrokes are required to initiate the first step of the download process. The user begins by entering command mode, and then specifies the *d* command to initiate download. Cs-console prompts for the name of a file, and copies the named file to the management computer. The sequence of commands listed below are used to download file *myfile*; user input is displayed in bold, and prompts emitted by the cs-console program are displayed in plain face.

CONTROL-@	Escape to command mode
(command mode) **d**	Download file to manager
file: **myfile**	Specify name of file to transfer

- *Move The Image Into The Back-end.* The software at Purdue uses the *Trivial File Transfer Protocol* (*TFTP*) to copy a file from the management computer into the memory of a back-end — the back-end acts as a TFTP client which contacts a TFTP server running on the management computer. For now, we assume that the back-end contains a copy of a *monitor* program that contains TFTP client code. To enter the monitor program, the user requests cs-console to send a BREAK condition on the console serial line. Once the monitor program responds, the user then instructs the monitor to boot a copy of the file. The sequence of commands is:

CONTROL-@	Escape to command mode
(command mode) **b**	Send BREAK to back-end
monitor> **b**	Load a copy of the image into memory and run it

- *Recovery And Reloading The Monitor.* The above sequence of commands assumes that whoever used the back-end previously left the monitor program loaded in memory and left the machine in an operational state. Unfortunately, some experiments fail. If an experimental operating system crashes, for example, a back-end may be left without a monitor program in memory. In such cases, the next user needs to recover the back-end and reload the monitor program. To do so, the user enters the following sequence of commands:

CONTROL-@	Escape to command mode
(command mode) **p**	Force reboot of the back-end†

In the current version of the lab, the *p* command causes a hardware reset of the back-end (almost the equivalent of a power cycle). Cs-console contacts a server on the lab management computer, which sends the appropriate command to the reset controller over a serial line. The reset controller then resets the back-end exactly as if a user pressed the hardware reset switch.

19.7 Automated Recovery

How does resetting the hardware force a back-end to run the monitor program? At various times, we have used two mechanisms. An early version of the lab used the back-end's console serial line — after resetting the computer, cs-console downloaded the monitor program over the serial line, and then started the CPU executing it. Later versions of the lab rely on the standard bootstrap hardware in a PC. We create a special boot disk that contains the monitor program, and insert a copy of the disk in the floppy drive of each back-end. When a hardware reset occurs, the hardware checks the floppy drive before checking the hard drive. When it finds a bootable disk in the floppy drive, the hardware loads the contents into memory, and branches to the beginning of the program. Thus, even if the previous user leaves the back-end CPU stopped and the memory empty, it is possible to recover the monitor program, which can then be used to reload and restart the back-end. More important, recovery can be carried out automatically from a remote location (i.e., without requiring a human to physically touch the back-end).

19.8 Organization Of The Lab Software

Two application programs form the core of lab management software: *cs-console* and *c-server*. We have already discussed the cs-console application. It provides the user interface through which all communication with back-end computers occurs. The user invokes cs-console in a window on a front-end computer, and then uses the window to control and communicate with a back-end computer.

As the name implies, the second of the two applications, *c-server*, operates as a server. C-server runs on the lab management computer, where it waits for contact from cs-console. C-server handles all the tasks of allocating a back-end, establishing communication with the back-end's console, moving an image from the front-end to a boot directory, and resetting the back-end.

---

†The mnemonic *p* stands for *power cycle* because the original scheme used to recover a back-end consisted of turning off the 110 VAC power, waiting five seconds, and turning the power back on.

Communication between cs-console and c-server uses both UDP and TCP — cs-console sends each individual command in a UDP message; TCP is used for communication with the back-end console. For example, when a user invokes it, cs-console sends a UDP command to c-server that requests a back-end be allocated. C-server performs several steps before sending a reply to cs-console. First, c-server allocates an unused back-end. Second, it establishes access to the back-end's console through the console multiplexor hardware. Third, c-server obtains an unused TCP port, creates a socket, and prepares to accept a connection. Fourth, it spawns a process that will handle console I/O. The spawned process is a server that waits for a connection on the chosen TCP port, and then passes data in both directions between the connection and the back-end. After spawning the extra process, c-server uses UDP to send a reply back to cs-console. Among other things, the reply specifies the TCP port at which the spawned process is waiting.

When it receives a reply, cs-console establishes a TCP connection to the TCP port specified in the reply. It then passes data in both directions between the TCP connection and the user's keyboard/screen. Thus, two applications and a TCP connection lie on the path between a user and a back-end console. When a user enters a keystroke, cs-console (running on the front-end) sends the character over the TCP connection. The console process (running on the lab management computer) receives the character from the TCP connection, and forwards the character through the console multiplexor to the back-end. Figure 19.3 illustrates the exchanges.

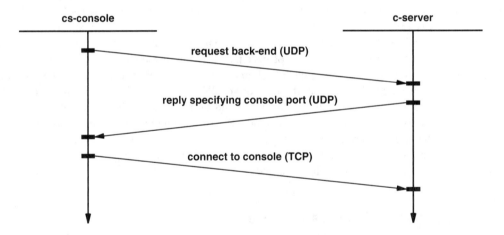

Figure 19.3 Illustration of the exchanges between cs-console and c-server, shown with time proceeding down the page. C-server handles UDP messages directly, but spawns a separate process to accept a TCP connection and handle console I/O.

What happens if a user allocates a back-end, and accidentally forgets to free it? C-server handles such situations. When it allocates a back-end, c-server starts a timer. The timer is reset whenever the user sends a character to the back-end console. If the user leaves the console connection idle more than K minutes (K is a parameter set by the lab administrator), the timer expires, and c-server releases the back-end.

19.9 Reset Controller Hardware

The reset controller is the most unusual piece of equipment in the lab because the hardware unit was custom built. Functionally, the reset controller provides a control path between lab software and the reset switch on each back-end computer. Physically, the controller connects to the lab management computer via a serial line; it connects to the reset switch on each back-end computer over a pair of dedicated wires. When a user needs to reset a back-end, the user enters a request to cs-console, which uses UDP to communicate the request to c-server. When it receives a reset request, c-server verifies that the user is authorized to make the request (i.e., owns the back-end), and then issues the commands to the reset controller that implement the request.

The reset controller contains three conceptual parts: a serial-to-parallel converter, a demultiplexor, and a set of solid-state relays. Figure 19.4 illustrates the organization.

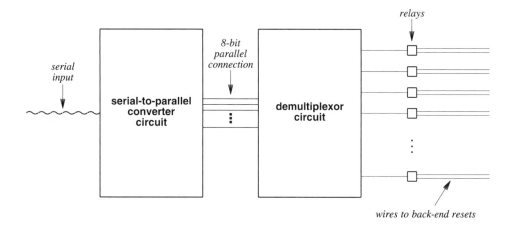

Figure 19.4 Conceptual organization of the reset controller. The input that arrives over a serial line is converted to parallel, and then used to activate one of the relays, which resets a back-end.

To understand the operation of the reset controller, you must know that the controller can only reset one back-end at any time. Think of each back-end as being assigned a number from 0 through *N-1*. Input to the controller consists of an 8-bit character that arrives over the serial line. The controller converts the input to a parallel form, treats it as an integer between 0 and 255, uses the integer to select one of the back-ends, and then resets that back-end. In fact, the controller merely triggers a solid-state relay, which is connected over a pair of wires to the back-end's reset switch. The effect is the same as if someone pressed the reset button on the back-end.

We said that c-server, which runs on the lab management computer, handles all back-end reset requests. When a request arrives, c-server must verify that the user who made the request is authorized to do so. Once the request is authorized, c-server converts the back-end computer ID to the corresponding 8-bit integer, and sends the integer over the serial line to the reset controller. As we have seen, the controller trips the corresponding relay, which causes a hardware reset on the back-end. Because it does not contain timers or cancellation logic, the reset controller does not automatically stop the relay. Instead, c-server must send the controller a second character to turn off the relay. The rebooter hardware is designed so that any input character not equal to the back-end's assigned value will reset the back-end's relay.

The chief advantage of the controller design is simplicity. Because software specifies exactly when to turn on or off a relay, the controller can be constructed from a few integrated circuits (chips). A single chip known as a *UART* performs the work of converting serial input to a parallel form. An additional chip known as a *latch* holds the value once the UART has finished conversion. The latch emits a parallel form of output that connects to a *demultiplexor* chip. The demultiplexor treats its input as an integer, and selects one of N possible output lines.

19.10 Scaling The Architecture

Does the architecture in Figure 19.1 scale? There are two primary issues: performance bottlenecks and physical interconnection limitations. For a reasonable number of computers, performance is not usually an issue because it is possible to upgrade the speed of the CPUs and the capacity of the network. Physical interconnections can become a bottleneck because each hardware device imposes limits on connections. For example, Ethernet technology was once a problem because early hubs were limited to 16 computers. Fortunately, Ethernet technology advanced quickly — vendors found ways to accommodate many computers on a single logical segment. Thus, the author's current lab has 26 front-end computers and 86 back-end computers, all of which connect to the lab network.

Another limitation arises from the console multiplexor because each device has a fixed number of serial ports. For example, the console multiplexor device used in the author's lab offers a maximum of 32 serial ports. To accommodate more than 32 back-end machines, multiple copies of the device are needed. Fortunately, vendors have anticipated the need for many serial connections, and provide a way to use multiple copies of the device at the same time. Each of the multiplexors is assigned a unique ID on the SCSI bus, meaning that there is no interference. Furthermore, driver software in the management computer is arranged to hide the underlying multiplexors. Thus, applications running in the management computer see a seamless set of 96 serial interfaces; an application does not know that they are divided among three physical devices.

Scaling the reset controller also poses a problem. The most difficult part to scale consists of the demux circuit that selects one of N output lines. A demux chip with K input pins must have 2^k output pins. Because hardware chips are limited in size, no single chip can support an arbitrary number of output lines. Furthermore, demux chips with more than 16 output lines are extremely expensive. Unfortunately, a design that uses many smaller demux chips to achieve a large number of outputs requires additional logic that feeds each input value to one of the demux chips at a time.

Our design for scaling the reset controller, which was first suggested by a hardware technician, consists of building multiple copies of the reset controller, and programming each to handle a subset of the back-ends. Each copy uses a 4-bit demultiplexor which results in 16 output lines. To distinguish among multiple copies, circuitry is added that causes a copy to respond to a range of input values. The first copy responds to values between zero and fifteen, the second responds to values between sixteen and thirty one, and so on. Figure 19.5 illustrates the design.

To make each copy of the reset controller respond to values in the specified range, a comparator is used. The comparator takes two 4-bit values as input, and produces a single bit of output that is true only when the inputs are identical. The figure shows that the comparator is wired to compare the four high-order bits of the input value to the four bits of an assigned ID. Output from the comparator is tied to the *enable* pin on the demultiplexor; the demultiplexor operates only if the comparison succeeds.

To understand how the scheme works, imagine that we first assign each copy of the controller an ID from the sequence 0, 1, 2,... 15. The assigned ID is configured into the controller hardware by entering the value into four switches on the board. Once each copy has an ID configured, the controllers are ready for use. All serial input lines are wired together, which means that all copies of the controller receive each character sent over the serial line. As the figure shows, the hardware converts an input from serial to parallel, and then divides the 8-bit value into two 4-bit values. It passes the four low-order bits to the input lines of the demultiplexor circuit, and passes the four high-order bits to the comparator. The comparator tests whether the four high-order bits from the input agree with the 4-bit ID value assigned to the controller. If so, the comparator enables the demultiplexor; otherwise, the demultiplexor remains inactive.

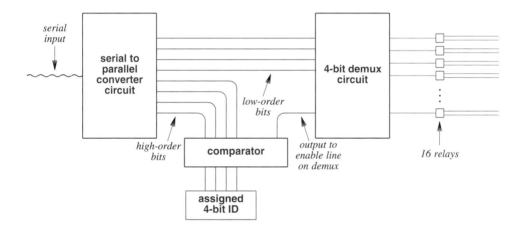

Figure 19.5 Illustration of the technique used to scale the reset controller. Each copy has a 4-bit value configured with switches.

Mathematically, we think of a command sent over the serial line as an 8-bit integer, with the high-order four bits selecting one copy of the controller and the low-order four bits selecting one of the sixteen output lines on that controller. Thus, the 8-bit value:

$$0\ \ 0\ \ 0\ \ 0\quad 0\ \ 0\ \ 1\ \ 1$$

selects relay number 3 on the controller that has ID 0. The 8-bit value

$$0 \quad 0 \quad 1 \quad 0 \quad \quad 0 \quad 1 \quad 0 \quad 1$$

selects relay number 5 on the controller that has ID 2, and

$$0 \quad 0 \quad 0 \quad 1 \quad \quad 0 \quad 0 \quad 0 \quad 0$$

selects relay number 0 on the controller that has ID 1.

Interestingly, the controller does not contain circuitry to turn off a relay. Instead, the controller relies on the arrival of another command to change its state. Turning off the relay is easy, however, because receipt of any value in which the two four bits differ from the assigned ID will disable the demultiplexor and turn off the relay. Thus, after sending a value to select a relay, we can send a large, unused value to reset it. For example, most labs will only have a few copies of the controller. In such cases, the value:

$$1 \quad 1 \quad 1 \quad 1 \quad \quad 0 \quad 0 \quad 0 \quad 0$$

can be used as a reset because it does not correspond to any controller ID.

19.11 Virtual Lab

The lab described in this chapter is designed to be virtual. That is, the lab is constructed in such a way that experimenters do not need to be physically present when they use the facilities. Instead, the lab can be accessed over the Internet. Front-end workstations have been given Internet access so an experimenter can use *telnet* or *ssh* to log into a front-end from anywhere on the Internet. The experimenter can then compile code or use cs-console to allocate, download, and interact with back-end computer(s). The reset controller even allows the experimenter to reset a back-end without being present.

Both administrators and users appreciate the virtual capability. To an individual, remote access makes a lab more convenient. Remote access allows the individual to run an experiment quickly, without spending any time commuting to the lab. More important, because the lab appears in a window, the experimenter can easily switch to tasks in other windows while waiting for code to compile. To a lab administrator, remote access makes better use of facilities because experiments are not restricted by the number of physical screens in the lab. Several experimenters can log into a single front-end and work simultaneously. One can be compiling and downloading, for example, while another interacts with a back-end.

19.12 Further Details

All the lab mangement software described in this chapter is available from:

http://www.netbook.cs.purdue.edu/labbook/Xinu-lab

A detailed schematic for the reset controller can be found at:

ftp://ftp.cs.purdue.edu/pub/comer/labbook/controller-schematic.ps

19.13 Summary

We have described a hardware and software architecture for a lab that supports protocol stack experiments. The architecture includes front-end computers that are used to compile and link an image and back-end computers that are used to test an image. A lab management computer runs servers that automate the tasks of downloading an image into a back-end, providing interactive access to the back-end console, and recovering a back-end after a system crashes. The architecture can scale to handle many front-ends and back-ends.

20

Protocol Stack Development Experiments

20.1 Introduction

Most of the experiments described in earlier chapters are designed so they can be solved in a relatively short time (e.g., a single lab session or at most a week of work). This chapter takes an entirely different approach by sketching experiments that are extremely broad. Each experiment requires a significant investment of time and energy, and will lie beyond the capabilities of someone who has just begun a study of networks and internets. In fact, the final experiment is the major project in the author's advanced graduate course on Internetworking.

20.2 The Value Of Building A Stack

Despite their difficulty, the experiments in this chapter are exciting. Instead of merely using or configuring TCP/IP software, the experiments ask you to implement parts of a protocol stack and verify that the code is both efficient and correct. The experiments force you to think about the overhead inherent in each software module, and look for ways to improve efficiency. In addition, the test of correctness is exacting — instead of arranging for two copies of your code to exchange datagrams, your stack is tested by having it interoperate with a commercial version of TCP/IP. That is, the resulting code must be able to exchange datagrams with systems that are used on the global Internet.

As you can imagine, building a protocol stack that can interact with a production version requires incredible attention to detail. One small mistake can cause datagrams to be rejected. Thus, in addition to the time spent programming, experiments in this chapter require extensive amounts of debugging. When you succeed in completing one of the projects, you will feel an immense sense of accomplishment and pride.

Ironically, although they are among the most difficult, the experiments described here are also most likely to be extended. Once you have built a protocol stack that can handle the basics, adding another protocol or another application is both straightforward and exciting. For example, once you succeed in building a stack that uses manual configuration, you can choose to experiment with auto-configuration using DHCP. Similarly, after an IP routing table has been built to forward unicast datagrams, multicast forwarding poses an intriguing challenge.

20.3 Summary

The experiments in this chapter require substantially more time, effort, and systems expertise than those in previous chapters — a single experiment can require many weeks (e.g., a semester). Despite their size and difficulty, the experiments engender enthusiasm and excitement.

Experiment 20.1
Interface With A Network Device Driver

Purpose

To learn how to interface with device driver software that controls a network interface device.

Background Reading And Preparation

Consult a general architecture text for information about DMA I/O devices. Read *Operating System Design — The Xinu Approach* for a description of Xinu device driver software, the interrupt mechanism, and buffer primitives.

Overview

Build a program that uses the Xinu operating system to read frames from an Ethernet into memory.

Procedure And Details (checkmark as each is completed)

_____ 1. Obtain a copy of the Xinu operating system code from:

> ftp://ftp.cs.purdue.edu/pub/Xinu

_____ 2. Add a main procedure that prints ''hello world'' on the console device.

_____ 3. Allocate a back-end computer, download the image into the back-end, and verify that it executes correctly.

_____ 4. Revise the main program so it uses the ETHER device to read a frame into memory. Dump the frame in hexadecimal to verify that you have correctly interfaced with the driver.

_____ 5. Modify the main program to allocate a buffer, and then iterate five times. For each iteration, read one frame from the *ETHER* device into the buffer, format the frame in hexadecimal, and display the results on the *CONSOLE*.

_____ 6. Modify the system so that instead of creating a process to run the main program, the system startup procedure calls function *ethread* to read a frame into memory. Dump the frame in hexadecimal to verify that you have correctly interfaced with the driver.

_____ 7. Modify your program to use the DMA facilities in the device driver for high-speed frame capture: allocate a set of buffers, and arrange for the driver to deposit frames in each buffer.

Optional Extensions (checkmark options as they are completed)

_____ 8. Add facilities to your program to display only those frames that contain an IP datagram. Display fields of the datagram header with appropriate labels (e.g., *SRC ADDR* and *DEST ADDR*).

_____ 9. Extend your code to function as a command (i.e., arrange for an application program to communicate with the driver). Add command-line arguments that allow a user to specify which frames should be displayed. (Hint: look at the packet analyzer in Experiment 12.4 for a few possibilities.)

_____ 10. Measure the performance of your code in packets-per-second that it can handle, and optimize the code to run at wire speed.

Notes

Name: _____

Experiment 20.2
Build An IP Forwarding Mechanism

Purpose

To learn how to build an IP routing table that is used to forward datagrams to the correct destination.

Background Reading And Preparation

Read *Internetworking With TCP/IP Volume 1: Principles, Protocols, and Architecture* for information about protocols such as ARP, IP, ICMP, and DHCP. Read *Internetworking With TCP/IP Volume 2: Design, Implementation, and Internals* for details about the Xinu implementation of TCP/IP, and consult RFCs for the official protocol standards.

Overview

Build and test an IP routing table that supports datagram forwarding with arbitrary address masks (i.e., full CIDR routes).

Procedure And Details (checkmark as each is completed)

_____ 1. Obtain, compile, and download a copy of the Xinu operating system that has TCP/IP support.

_____ 2. Devise a data structure for an IP routing table that can accommodate arbitrary address masks. If designed correctly, the data structure should allow the full range of possibilities, including network-specific, subnet-specific, or host-specific routes.

_____ 3. Implement the data structure in Xinu (i.e., replace the current routing table).

_____ 4. Test the resulting system for correctness. Load the routing table with a conventional set of destination routes, look up destination addresses, and display the results on the console.

_____ 5. Test special cases such as a default route and directed broadcast addresses.

_____ 6. Measure the speed of your implementation in lookups per second.

_____ 7. Extend the test by using your routing table to perform forwarding of datagrams among multiple networks.

Optional Extensions (checkmark options as they are completed)

_____ 8. A routing table that contains pointers must be locked during update to ensure that IP does not attempt datagram forwarding while the table is in an inconsistent state. Unfortunately, locking decreases the average lookup speed. Devise an optimized version of the routing table that avoids locking by using two copies of the table. At any time, use one copy for lookups and one to modify routes. When a modification is complete, switch the two copies.

_____ 9. Measure the lookup speed of your implementation for twenty sizes ranging from 2 entries to 30,000 entries, and plot the performance.

Notes

Experiment 20.3
Implement An IP Router

Purpose

To learn how to implement the protocols used in an IP router.

Background Reading And Preparation

Read *Internetworking With TCP/IP Volume 1: Principles, Protocols, and Architecture* for information about protocols such as ARP, IP, ICMP, RIP, and DHCP. Read *Internetworking With TCP/IP Volume 2: Design, Implementation, and Internals* for details about the Xinu implementation of TCP/IP, and consult RFCs for the official protocol standards.

Overview

Build an IP router that connects three networks and forwards datagrams among them. Implement ARP, IP, ICMP, and RIP.

Procedure And Details (checkmark as each is completed)

_____ 1. Begin with a copy of the Xinu operating system used in the Xinu Lab at Purdue that has emulation support for multiple network interfaces. Choose a unique ID for your router from 1, 2, 3, and so on, and use the ID to allow the emulation software to assign IP and MAC addresses to the three networks that connect to your router.

_____ 2. Implement ARP software.

_____ 3. Replace the Xinu ARP code with yours, and test the result.

_____ 4. Implement a basic IP module that includes a CIDR routing table and forwards datagrams.

_____ 5. Replace the Xinu IP code with yours, and test the result.

_____ 6. Add fragmentation and reassembly to your IP code.

_____ 7. Integrate your new code into Xinu, and test the result.

_____ 8. Implement ICMP.

_____ 9. Replace the Xinu ICMP code with yours, and test the result.

_____ 10. Implement version 2 of RIP.

_____ 11. Replace the Xinu RIP code with yours, and test the result.

_____ 12. Add DHCP client support to your IP code.

_____ 13. Test the resulting system by using it in both a router and a host.

Optional Extensions (checkmark options as they are completed)

_____ 14. Implement and test Path MTU Discovery.

_____ 15. Add support for IGMP, and build a chat application that uses multicast to deliver datagrams.

_____ 16. Extend your router to handle Network Address Translation. Test your NAT code by using your router to connect a private network to the global Internet.

Notes

Part VI
Network Component Design
In An Engineering Lab

Experiments With The Design And Implementation Of High-Speed Network Equipment
That Can Be Carried Out In A Network System Engineering Lab

21

Hardware And Software For A Network System Engineering Lab

The previous section discusses a lab that supports the implementation of protocol software on conventional hardware. Although a low-end component, such as an IP router with two Ethernet interfaces, may use a software implementation of protocols, higher-speed requires specialized hardware. This section explores one of the technologies that engineers use to build higher-speed network equipment: network processors. The current chapter describes the hardware and software needed in a lab that allows experimentation with network processors. The next chapter outlines experiments that are possible in such a lab.

21.1 Network Processors

For many years, networking equipment fell into two categories. Vendors began building network systems with conventional computer hardware (i.e., CPU, memory, and bus), and implemented protocol processing in software. Later generations of network hardware use customized integrated circuits called *Application Specific ICs* (*ASICs*). Conventional hardware has the advantages of low cost and flexibility; ASIC designs have the advantage of high speed. Recently, chip manufacturers have developed *network processor* technology to provide a middle ground. On one hand, a network processor resembles a conventional CPU because it is programmable. Because software can be replaced, a design that uses network processors can be upgraded without requiring completely new hardware. Thus, programmability means that a network processor retains the advantages of lower cost and easier modification found in conventional computer hardware. On the other hand, a network processor offers higher speed than a conventional computer. Network processors achieve the high speed through the use of parallel processing and an instruction set that is optimized for protocol processing.

Many vendors are developing network processors. Some vendors have developed special-purpose network processors to use in their own products; chip vendors sell general-purpose network processors to many companies. Consequently, some network processors are designed to handle a specific task (e.g., forwarding frames in an Ethernet switch), while other network processors are designed to be general enough to use in a variety of ways. Although a few network processors have support for specific protocols (e.g., IP datagram reassembly), most contain an instruction set that is sufficiently general to allow them to be used with a variety of protocols.

21.2 Facilities Needed

What lab facilities are needed to conduct experiments with network processors? It may seem that hardware experiments require interconnecting chips (i.e., wire wrapping or soldering). In the case of network processors, however, their programmability makes it possible to experiment without changing the physical interconnections. Instead, a general-purpose hardware configuration can be used for many experiments. For example, imagine a configuration that includes one or more network processors, memory, one or more I/O interfaces (e.g., for Ethernet), and all the necessary interconnections (e.g., a bus). To use such a configuration, the experimenter downloads a program into the network processor's memory, and starts the processor running. The experimenter can then observe the resulting system as it forwards packets. When one experiment ends, new code can be downloaded into the network processor, and a new experiment can begin.

Many similarities exist between the lab facilities needed to support network processor experiments and the lab facilities for protocol development described in Chapter 19. Both labs require experimenters to create and test software that processes packets. In each case, the experimenter must compile and link the software to produce a binary image, which is then downloaded into the target hardware for execution. Furthermore, in each case, the binary image must take complete control of the processor on which it runs. The similarities make it reasonable to follow the same general approach in each lab. That is, two types of hardware are needed: front-end machines used to prepare programs and back-end machines used to test programs.

21.3 Hardware For An Example Lab

To illustrate the facilities needed in a network system engineering lab, we will describe the architecture of a laboratory that uses Intel network processors†. As in a protocol development lab, conventional workstations serve as front-end computers. The front-end computers, which are connected by a network, run a standard operating system (e.g., Linux) that provides a stable, production environment. Front-ends are used for software preparation and downloading. Thus, a front-end workstation needs a specialized set of tools that allow an experimenter to write, cross-compile, and cross-link code that will eventually run on a network processor. In addition, the front-end system needs software that allows an experimenter to download the resulting image into a network processor and then control the processor.

---

†The author gratefully acknowledges support for the lab from Intel Corporation.

The main difference between a system engineering lab and the protocol development lab described in the previous section lies in the back-end hardware. In a protocol development lab, the back-end hardware consists of conventional computers connected to a network. Each computer includes a BIOS and a conventional hardware bootstrap facility that can be used to load code into memory and start the computer. In contrast, highly specialized back-end hardware is required for a network system engineering lab. Besides a network processor and the associated connections to a power source, the hardware must include a memory subsystem and I/O interfaces. The configuration must be sufficiently realistic to permit testing, and sufficiently general to accommodate a variety of experiments. Finally, the hardware must include a mechanism that allows an experimenter to load a program into the back-end memory and start the network processor executing.

21.4 A Network Processor Testbed

How can a hardware testbed facility be constructed? Many vendors chose a straightforward scheme to use with their network processors: create a reference system that contains the necessary hardware components (network processor plus memory and Ethernet interfaces) into a reference system, and make it available commercially. For example, Intel Corporation offers a single printed circuit board that contains an IXP network processor plus four Ethernet ports. To simplify communication between the front-end computer and the board, the board is designed to plug into a PCI bus. That is, from the front-end's point of view, the board appears to be a special-purpose system connected to the bus. Figure 21.1 illustrates the conceptual organization.

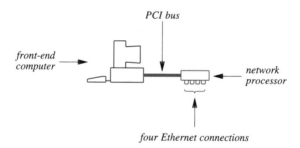

Figure 21.1 The conceptual organization of a network processor testbed used by Intel Corporation for their IXP1200.

The front-end computer communicates with the board over the PCI bus (e.g., to download software or start the network processor). When it runs an experiment, the board can operate independent of the front-end because the network processor can use the four Ethernet ports to send and receive frames.

Physically, Intel's network processor board plugs into a bus slot like any other I/O interface board (i.e., the board is located inside the front-end computer). The chief advantage of plugging into a bus arises from hardware savings — the board does not need an external power supply because electrical power can be obtained directly from the bus.

21.5 Software For The Example Lab

What software is needed for a network processor lab like the one described above? Three basic items are required:

- *Device Driver.* The most essential piece of software consists of a module that provides communication between an application program running on the PC and the network processor board. Because a network processor board functions like an I/O device, the communication software is written in the form of a *device driver* that is embedded in the operating system. All communication between an application running on the PC and the network processor hardware goes through the device driver.

- *Cross-Development Software.* The front-end needs tools such as an editor, compiler, assembler, and linker that allow an experimenter to create software for the network processor. The tools are known as *cross-development tools* because the target architecture differs from the architecture on which the tools run. That is, the tools run on the front-end (i.e., a conventional PC), but produce code for a network processor (i.e., a device with an unusual instruction set).

- *Download And Control Software.* The front-end needs software that provides a user interface to the back-end. The software handles two activities: it allows an experimenter to download code into the network processor's memory and control the network processor (i.e., start or stop execution). Typically, the download and control software is implemented by one or more application programs that use the device driver to communicate with the back-end.

Vendors use a variety of terms for the software described in this chapter. Intel Corporation uses the term *Software Development Kit* (*SDK*) to refer to the software they supply for the IXP1200 testbed. The SDK includes both cross-development tools and control software. Other vendors use slight variations in the terminology.

21.6 Relationship To Previous Lab Architectures

Because the board containing a network processor can be embedded in a conventional workstation, the facilities described in this chapter need not be exclusive. In particular, when they are not being used to experiment with network processors, the front-end workstations can be used for other purposes. For example, if they are connected by a network, the front-end workstations can be used for network programming experiments as described in Part II of this text, for network measurement experiments as described in Part III, or for configuration experiments described in Part IV. The author has chosen to use the front-ends as part of the protocol development lab described in Part V.

It may seem that experimenters can use the network systems lab from a remote location. Indeed, because each front-end workstation attaches to the Internet and runs a conventional operating system, an experimenter can use *telnet* or *ssh* to log into a workstation from a remote site. Once they log in, experimenters can access the cross-development and download software. However, each network processor board has four Ethernet ports that must each be connected to a device that can send or receive traffic. To automate the connection, our lab has been extended to incorporate a VLAN switch.

21.7 Summary

Network processors are programmable hardware devices used to implement packet processing systems such as IP routers. To support experimentation with network processors, a laboratory needs conventional front-end computers that run cross-development software and special-purpose back-end systems that each consist of a network processor, memory, and I/O devices. The experimenter uses a front-end to compile and download software to a network processor, and then observes the network processor as it handles packets.

Intel uses a straightforward mechanism to permit experimentation with their IXP1200 network processor: the processor, memory, and I/O devices are arranged on a board. As an optimization, the network processor board plugs into the PCI bus on a conventional PC. The PC can communicate with the board directly over the bus, permitting applications running on the PC to download and control the network processor.

22

Network Systems Engineering Experiments

22.1 Introduction

The previous chapter describes a network systems engineering lab that uses testbed facilities for network processors available from vendors. This chapter discusses experiments that can be conducted in such a lab. The experiments are written to assume that the lab uses Intel's IXP testbed and the associated Software Development Kit that includes a cross-compiler and download facilities. Although similar experiments may be possible with facilities from other vendors, the details will differ.

Many of the experiments seem straightforward, and some may seem trivial. However, because a network processor offers a low-level, embedded environment, programming such devices is not easy. Even a trivial task such as reading a packet presents a significant challenge — a network processor must transfer individual blocks of the packet from the framing hardware, and the transfer may involve intermediate hardware between the framer and memory. Thus, the experiments can take considerable time and effort.

22.2 Summary

This chapter describes a set of experiments for an Intel network processor. Because a network processor includes low-level hardware facilities, even simple tasks can require substantial effort.

Experiment 22.1

Configure Your Account

Purpose

To set up your account so you can program a network processor.

Background Reading And Preparation

Read documentation for account configuration specific to your lab.

Overview

Download network processor support software, and configure a computer account that allows you to compile a simple network processor application.

Procedure And Details (checkmark as each is completed)

_____ 1. Obtain and read the instructions for configuring your personal account to compile network processor applications.

_____ 2. Obtain a copy of the software source files necessary to build network processor applications for your network processor. Extract the files from the archive, and place them in your personal directory.

_____ 3. Configure your environment variables and start-up scripts according to the specific instructions for your facility.

_____ 4. Compile a simple network processor application to test that your development environment is configured correctly.

Optional Extensions (checkmark options as they are completed)

_____ 5. To verify that your environment is set up correctly, compile a variety of network processor applications that use each of the development tools (e.g., a C compiler, microassembler, linker).

_____ 6. Modify a file by adding a comment, and run *make* to verify that the file is recompiled (or reassembled).

Notes

Experiment 22.2

Compile And Download Code To A Network Processor

Purpose

To learn how to compile network processor applications, download them to a network processor, and test applications using lab facilities.

Background Reading And Preparation

Read the directions on compiling a network processor application and accessing a network processor in your lab. Also consult your lab instructor to learn how to send packets to the network processor.

Overview

Intel's SDK includes examples of code that can be downloaded into the network processor. Intel uses the term *Active Computing Element* (*ACE*) to describe a downloadable module, and the term *microACE* to describe a downloadable module that includes code for both the microengine and RISC processor components of the IXP†. Compile the sample microACE software that counts packets, load the resulting object code onto a network processor, and test the result by sending packets to the network processor.

Procedure And Details (checkmark as each is completed)

_____ 1. Find the microACE for a simple network processor application that counts packets on a network.

_____ 2. Compile the packet counting application.

_____ 3. Use the SDK facilities to download the resulting object code onto a network processor board along with the necessary configuration files.

---

†The IXP architecture includes a conventional RISC CPU plus special-purpose CPUs called *microengines* that are used to process packets.

_____ 4. Configure your network so you can send packets to the network processor.

_____ 5. Run the packet count application, and transmit packets to the network processor. Verify that the network processor counts the correct number of packets. Note: if using standard TCP/IP to generate packets, you must establish ARP entries in the counting ACE (see file *ixsys.config*).

Optional Extensions (checkmark options as they are completed)

_____ 6. Download other network processor applications supplied by the vendor such as a Layer 2 bridge.

_____ 7. Stress test the packet count application by flooding the network with as many packets as possible. How well does the application keep up with the network traffic?

Notes

Experiment 22.3
Build A Packet Analyzer On A Network Processor

Purpose

To learn how to build a packet analyzer on a network processor.

Background Reading And Preparation

Review Ethernet, IP, and TCP headers (Chapters 9, 20, and 25 in *Computer Networks and Internets* and IETF RFCs 791 and 793).

Overview

Build an application that captures packets from the network and analyzes them.

Procedure And Details (checkmark as each is completed)

_____ 1. Write an application that reads a set of packets and analyzes them. When a user enters the command *send_command summary* while logged into the network processor, the application should produce the following summary†:

> Layer 2 Summary (Ethernet)
>
> Total number of frames processed
> Average frame size (excluding header)
> Number and percentage of broadcast frames
> Number and percentage of multicast frames
> Number and percentage of unicast frames
> Number and percentage of each of the top five frame types

---

†See the simplified API manual for instructions on how to program your ACE to handle input from the *send_command* program.

Layer 3 Summary (IP)

Total number of datagrams processed
Average datagram size (excluding header)
Number and percentage of datagram fragments
Number and percentage of datagrams sent to network broadcast address
Number and percentage of datagrams sent to limited broadcast
Number and percentage of datagrams carrying TCP
Number and percentage of datagrams carrying UDP
Number and percentage of datagrams carrying ICMP

Layer 4 Summary (TCP)

Total number of TCP segments processed
Average segment size (excluding header)
Number and percentage of acknowledgements (no data)
Number and percentage of data segments
Number and percentage of SYN/FIN segments
Number and percentage of each of top five destination ports
Number and percentage of each of top five source ports

_____ 2. Use two computers and a network processor to test the application. Connect the two computers and the network processor to a private LAN. Generate traffic between the computers using applications such as telnet, ping and traceroute. Use tcpdump or an equivalent program to capture the traffic and check that your application produces the correct output.

_____ 3. Modify the application so that it can display the headers of the packets it analyzes. When a user enters the command *send_command verbose*, the application should display the contents of each header field (i.e., Ethernet, IP and TCP) for each packet received. When the user enters the command *send_command quiet*, the analyzer should revert to collecting statistics without displaying details.

Optional Extensions (checkmark options as they are completed)

_____ 4. Modify the application to take arguments that specify which packets to examine. When a user enters a command of the form *send_command filter <pattern>*, the application only analyzes (and displays if in verbose mode) packets that match the pattern. Devise patterns that limit the analyzer to a specific protocol (e.g., use the pattern *-ip* to limit analysis to IP packets). Devise additional patterns that allow a user to select frames sent by a specific computer or to a specific address. Use the command *send_command no-filter* to eliminate a previous pattern and resume analysis of all frames.

_____ 5. Extend your program to allow boolean combinations of pattern options. For example, it should be possible to limit processing to ARP frames or frames carrying IP that also contain TCP.

Notes

Experiment 22.4
Build An Ethernet Bridge

Purpose

To learn how to forward Ethernet frames according to the Ethernet bridging algorithm.

Background Reading And Preparation

Read Section 5.8 of *Network Systems Design Using Network Processors* to learn about the bridge algorithm.

Overview

Use a simplified network processor API to build an application that bridges two Ethernet segments.

Procedure And Details (checkmark as each is completed)

_____ 1. Obtain a copy of the code that passes all packets to the embedded processor.

_____ 2. Build an application for the embedded processor that forwards packets between two Ethernet ports (i.e., when it receives a frame on one port, the application sends the packet out the other port).

_____ 3. Connect two ports on the network processor to two Ethernet hubs, and connect a host to each hub. Verify that your application works by running *ping*, *telnet*, or *traceroute* between the two hosts.

_____ 4. Add a module to your application that extracts the Ethernet source address from each frame and builds a table of Ethernet addresses along with the port over which the address arrived. Arrange for the application to display the contents of the table on the console when a user enters *send_command showtable*.

_____ 5. Modify your application so it only forwards Ethernet frames according to the Ethernet briding algorithm. Be sure to handle broadcast and multicast frames correctly.

_____ 6. Connect two ports on the network processor to two Ethernet hubs. Connect two hosts to one hub, and a third host to the other hub. Send traffic between the three hosts. Use an application such as *ethereal* or *tcpdump* to verify that your bridge is forwarding traffic correctly.

Optional Extensions (checkmark options as they are completed)

_____ 7. Physically move a host from one segment to another, and verify that your bridge learns the new location.

_____ 8. Extend your bridge to forward traffic among more than two Ethernet ports (e.g., extend the bridge to use four Ethernet segments).

_____ 9. Implement the Distributed Spanning Tree protocol that detects and avoids loops.

_____ 10. To stress test your bridge, arrange for a high-speed host or packet generator to send back-to-back packets. Determine the number of packets your bridge can handle per second.

Notes

Experiment 22.5
Build An IP Fragmenter

Purpose

To learn how to fragment IP datagrams on a network processor.

Background Reading And Preparation

Read Section 5.9 in *Network Systems Design Using Network Processors* for information on IP fragmentation and reassembly. Consult RFC 791 to learn the details of IP header fields used in fragmentation and RFC 815 for information on reassembly.

Overview

Construct and test a network processor application that fragments IP datagrams.

Procedure And Details (checkmark as each is completed)

_____ 1. Use the simplified network processor API to create an application that forwards frames between two Ethernet ports. Arrange for the application to forward all frames except IP datagrams that are larger than some fixed MTU (e.g., 128). (Note: do not count the Ethernet header when computing the size of the IP datagram.) The application should drop frames containing IP packets that exceed the chosen MTU. Allow a user to set the MTU value with the *send_command* application.

_____ 2. Modify your application so that instead of dropping IP frames that exceed the (artificial) MTU, the code fragments the datagrams according to IP fragmentation rules. Your application should be able to handle fragmentation for a frame that contains a complete IP datagram or a frame that contains a previously fragmented datagram.

_____ 3. Test your application by connecting two hosts to independent Ethernet hubs and connecting those Ethernet hubs to the network processor. Send large IP or UDP packets from one host to the other using either *ping*, *netcat*, or an equivalent program, and verify that the packets are received properly on the destination host.

_____ 4. Send packets of various sizes including: packets smaller than the MTU of both the Ethernet and the fragmenter, packets smaller than the Ethernet MTU (i.e., 1500 octets) but larger than the fragmenter MTU, and packets larger than both MTUs.

_____ 5. Change the MTU of your fragmenter application, and test the application again. Use a monitoring program that measures the resulting packet size to verify that the application produces packets for the specified MTU.

Optional Extensions (checkmark options as they are completed)

_____ 6. Extend your application so it sends the appropriate ICMP message back to the source host when a datagram needs fragmentation and the *DO NOT FRAGMENT* bit is set. Verify that your application sends the ICMP message and drops the original datagram.

_____ 7. Arrange for your application to prevent further fragmentation. When it fragments a datagram, have the application set the *DO NOT FRAGMENT* bit in the datagram. Arrange for the application to monitor ICMP traffic, and report occurrences of ICMP *Destination Unreachable* messages that have a *Code* value equal to *4* (such messages mean that fragmentation was required, but the *DO NOT FRAGMENT* bit was set). Verify that your application works by forwarding traffic to a router that is configured with a small MTU.

_____ 8. Extend the previous exercise to implement *Path MTU Discovery*. If an ICMP message arrives that indicates fragmentation was required, increase the MTU size for subsequent datagrams.

_____ 9. Create a network processor application that performs IP reassembly.

Experiment 22.6
Build A Traffic Classifier

Purpose

To learn about optimized traffic classification and classification languages.

Background Reading And Preparation

Read Chapter 16 of *Network Systems Design Using Network Processors* to learn about classification languages. Determine which classification language to use for this lab.

Overview

Create network processor code that classifies packets according to the data they carry up through application layer protocols.

Procedure And Details (checkmark as each is completed)

_____ 1. Write network processor code to classify incoming packets into each of the following categories, labeling each packet with the specified numeric tag. Have the network processor drop packets that do not fall into the specified classes. If a packet falls into more than one class, place it in the class with the lowest number.

Description	Tag
Any IP datagram to 10.1.2.3	1
TCP control (SYN/FIN/RST) to/from port 21	2
TCP control (SYN/FIN/RST) to/from port 22	3
TCP control (SYN/FIN/RST) to/from port 25	4
TCP control (SYN/FIN/RST) to/from port 80	5
TCP bulk data	6
RIP requests	7
UDP to port 139	8
UDP	9
ICMP	10
IP with options	11
ARP	12

_____ 2. Augment your classifier program so that it reports packets and their classifications as it receives them.

_____ 3. Create test traffic that contains packets in each of the above traffic classes. To verify that your classifier handles ambiguous traffic, include packets that belong to two or more classes.

_____ 4. Load your classifier onto a network processor, and send the packets you generated in the previous step to the network processor. Verify that your program classifies each packet correctly.

Optional Extensions (checkmark options as they are completed)

_____ 5. Stress test your classifier by transmitting large volumes of packets at high speed. Verify that your code operates fast enough to avoid dropping packets.

_____ 6. Extend your classifier by adding explicit rules that use values in the header to determine whether to drop or forward packets in each class (i.e., build a simple *firewall*).

_____ 7. Modify your classifier so that Class 1 also includes packets destined to a specified set of IP addresses. Allow the set of IP addresses to be changed at runtime.

Experiment 22.7
Create A Minimal MicroACE

Purpose

Learn how to create a basic microACE.

Background Reading And Preparation

Read Chapters 22 through 24 of *Network Systems Design Using Network Processors* to learn about microACEs and how they are programmed. Read the Intel Programmer's Reference Manual to learn about the microcode used with the Intel network processor.

Overview

Construct a microACE that counts frames.

Procedure And Details (checkmark as each is completed)

_____ 1. Obtain a basic microACE example from your lab instructor. The example code contains all necessary initialization, but the code merely drops each frame that arrives. The core component of the example code includes a mechanism that can receive commands from an application. Study the example to learn how the code is structured and how it operates.

_____ 2. Compile, downlaod, and test the example code.

_____ 3. Modify the microengine component so that instead of dropping all frames, the code raises an *exception* (i.e., passes each frame to the core component).

_____ 4. Modify the core component to count the number of frames that arrive as exceptions. Arrange for the core component to display the count of frames when it receives a request from a command-line application. Note: after counting a frame, the core component should drop the frame.

_____ 5. Test your packet counting ACE by connecting a port on the network processor to an Ethernet hub and using another computer to generate traffic on the hub. Verify that your ACE code correctly counts packets.

Optional Extensions (checkmark options as they are completed)

_____ 6. Create your own cross-call mechanism to allow arbitrary applications to retrieve the frame count from your microACE.

_____ 7. Extend the microACE so that each frame is counted by the microengines instead of the core component. To permit the core component to display the count, the value should be kept in memory that is shared by both the microengines and the core processor.

_____ 8. Extend the microengine-based counting mechanism from the previous exercise to count each type of packet (e.g., IP, ARP, TCP, or UDP).

Notes

Experiment 22.8
Create A Classifier Microblock

Purpose

Learn to analyze packets in microcode.

Background Reading And Preparation

Read Chapter 25 in *Network Systems Design Using Network Processors* for an overview of microcode. See Chapter 26 for an example ACE. Also read the Intel Programmer's Reference manual for microcode specifics.

Overview

Create a microblock that classifies packets according to their network headers.

Procedure And Details (checkmark as each is completed)

_____ 1. Create a microblock that uses the Intel Dispatch Loop macros to examine and classify each frame. Use the header fields to divide frames into five classes. The microblock should consist of two macros : Classify_Init[] and Classify[]. The Classify[] macro is called for each frame, and must set its argument register to the class of the frame. The Classify_Init[] macro is called once; it must initialize any global data structures needed for Classify[]. The classes are:

Class	Eth Src Port	IP?	TCP to Port 80?	SYN|FIN|RST?
1	1 or 2	X	X	X
2	0	NO	X	X
3	0	YES	NO	X
4	0	YES	YES	NO
5	0	YES	YES	YES

_____ 2. Obtain a sample microACE from your lab instructor. The dispatch loop in the sample code calls the Classify microblock, and the core component displays the first 60 octets of each frame along with the exception code for each frame it receives.

_____ 3. Assemble the microACE with your microblock.

_____ 4. Test your code by attaching ports 0, 1 and 2 of your network processor to three separate Ethernet LANs and generating traffic on each. Use the frame headers displayed by the core component to verify that the value returned by your Classify[] macro is correct.

Optional Extensions (checkmark options as they are completed)

_____ 5. Extend the microblock to match arbitrary patterns in the header of each frame. Have the microblock read the patterns from memory.

_____ 6. Extend the previous exercise to read the patterns from scratch memory before testing each frame header. Modify the core component to accept patterns via a crosscall and install the pattern into scratch memory at runtime.

Notes

Experiment 22.9
Build Microengine Frame Forwarding Code

Purpose

To learn how to forward packets in a microblock.

Background Reading And Preparation

Read about transmitting frames in microcode on the Intel network processor in Sections 25.14 and 25.15 of *Network Systems Design Using Network Processors*. See Chapter 26 for an example ACE. Also read the Intel Programmer's Reference Guide for microcode details.

Overview

Create a microACE that forwards packets according to a classification tag.

Procedure And Details (checkmark as each is completed)

_____ 1. Learn how to use microcode to modify the destination port of a frame.

_____ 2. Create microcode for a dispatch loop that runs a microblock and uses a return value to determine the next action. Follow the Intel convention of using register *dl_next_block* for the return value.

dl_next_block	Action
IX_BUFFER_NULL	Drop
1	Set Dst Port to 0; send to next microblock.
2	Raise frame as exception #1.
3	Set Dst Port to 1; send to next microblock.
4	Set Dst Port to 2; send to next microblock.
5	Raise frame as exception #2.

_____ 3. Create a core exception handler that performs one of two actions on the exception code as
listed in the table below.

Exception Code	Action
1	Copy the frame. Set the Dst Port of the first copy to 1, and the second copy to 2. Send each frame to the default target.
2	Set the Dst Port to 2. Send the frame to the default target.

_____ 4. Obtain a microACE that sets register *dl_next_block* according to a Classify[] macro. Insert your microcode into the dispatch loop after the Classify[] macro and your exception
handler in place of the default exception handler of the microACE's core component.

_____ 5. Compile and download the microACE. Connect a network processor to three separate
Ethernet hubs, and generate traffic on each hub. Verify that your code classifies and forwards frames correctly.

Optional Extensions (checkmark options as they are completed)

_____ 6. Create your own classifier microblock (see Lab 22.6), and use it in place of the microACE shell.

_____ 7. Extend the exception handling code for type 2 exceptions so that it maintains state about
open web connections that pass across the network processor. Have the ACE report the
number of open web connections via a crosscall.

Index